Elizabeth Cady Stanton

The Right Is Ours

OXFORD
PORTRAITS

Elizabeth Cady Stanton

The Right Is Ours

Harriet Sigerman

OXFORD
UNIVERSITY PRESS

To my father, Leon Sigerman, who never doubted that a daughter could be everything a son could be.

OXFORD
UNIVERSITY PRESS

Oxford   New York
Athens Auckland Bangkok Bogotá   Buenos Aires   Cape Town
Chennai Dar es Salaam Delhi Florence   Hong Kong Istanbul Karachi
Kolkata Kuala Lumpur Madrid Melbourne Mexico City Mumbai Nairobi
Paris São Paulo Shanghai Singapore Taipei Tokyo Toronto Warsaw
and associated companies in Berlin   Ibadan

Copyright © 2001 by Harriet Sigerman
Published by Oxford University Press, Inc.
198 Madison Avenue, New York, New York 10016
www.oup.com

Design: Greg Wozney
Layout: Alexis Siroc
Picture research: Fran Antmann

Library of Congress Cataloging-in-Publication Data
Sigerman, Harriet.
Elizabeth Cady Stanton : the right is ours / Harriet Sigerman.
p. cm. -- (Oxford portraits)
Includes bibliographical references and index.
Summary: A biography of one of the first leaders of the women's rights
movement, whose work led to women's right to vote.
ISBN 0-19-511969-X
1. Stanton, Elizabeth Cady, 1815-1902--Juvenile literature. 2. Feminists--
United States--Juvenile literature. 3. Women's rights--United States--
History--Juvenile literature. [1. Stanton, Elizabeth Cady, 1815-1902. 2.
Suffragists. 3. Women's rights. 4. Women--Suffrage. 5. Women--Biography.]
I. Title. II. Series.

HQ1413.S67 S54 2001
305.42'092--dc21
[B]   2001031404
                 8506

9 8 7 6 5 4 3 2 1

Printed in the United States of America
on acid-free paper

On the cover: Elizabeth Cady Stanton in 1871, age 56
Frontispiece: Elizabeth Cady Stanton in her New York City apartment in 1901

CONTENTS

PROLOGUE: "THE ELEMENTS HAD CONSPIRED TO IMPEL ME ONWARD"

On the morning of July 11, 1848, Elizabeth Cady Stanton traveled to Waterloo, New York, three miles west of her home in Seneca Falls, to visit her good friend Lucretia Mott. Stanton had first met Mott, a Quaker and well-known antislavery activist, eight years before in London at the World's Anti-Slavery Convention; Stanton had attended the convention with her husband, Henry, while on their honeymoon. Both Mott and Stanton were very committed to the antislavery cause, which drew hundreds of American women into its ranks. Female members circulated petitions to abolish slavery, raised funds to pay for the freedom of runaway slaves, attended regional conventions, and wrote and lectured on the evils of slavery. Their tireless efforts resulted in the freedom of scores of slaves and helped galvanize Northerners' opposition to slavery.

But, to the astonishment of Mott and Stanton, a debate over allowing women to participate in the proceedings in London dominated the opening session of the convention. After several hours, the delegates who opposed women's participation prevailed. These delegates expressed the traditional view that woman's place was demurely in the home as wife and mother, not in the noisy public arena of reform and politics. As Elizabeth Cady Stanton and Lucretia Mott walked out of the hall together, stunned that the most liberal and enlightened reformers in the world would dare to silence their female comrades, they vowed to hold a convention as soon as they returned to America to proclaim women's rights.

Now, eight years later, they still had not organized such a convention. Although the two women had corresponded with each other in the intervening years, neither one had taken any action to fulfill the promise made in London. For her part, Elizabeth Cady Stanton had been preoccupied with the pleasures and responsibilities of being a wife and mother. Her first son, Daniel, was born in 1842, and two more sons, Henry and Gerrit, followed over the next three years. She took great joy in being a mother and was happily immersed in the many responsibilities of keeping a house.

From 1844 to 1847, the Stantons had lived in Boston, at that time the cultural and intellectual capital of America. When she was not preoccupied with household duties, Elizabeth Cady Stanton attended lectures and readings and socialized with an exciting circle of reformers and thinkers—intellectual giants like the poet and essayist Ralph Waldo Emerson; the brilliant minister Theodore Parker; and Frederick Douglass, a former slave and a powerful orator and newspaper editor.

But now her life was very different. In 1847, the Stantons moved to Seneca Falls, a quiet country village nestled in the beautiful Finger Lakes region of western New

Elizabeth Cady Stanton, photographed with her sons Henry and Daniel in about 1848, believed that being a mother helped her to better understand the domestic constraints in women's lives. This understanding shaped her thoughts about women's rights—especially her advocacy of birth control, divorce reform, and property rights for women.

York. The damp climate of Boston had not agreed with Henry Stanton's health, and his career prospects in law and politics had dwindled in Boston. When his father-in-law offered them a house in Seneca Falls, Henry Stanton decided to move. Seneca Falls offered none of the intellectual and cultural richness of Boston, and Elizabeth Stanton found her new neighbors to be friendly but narrow-minded.

Because she could not find suitable servants and her family had expanded, she also had to confront the difficult chores of housekeeping and full-time child raising on her own. Dust from the unpaved street in front of her house kept the floors and furniture permanently dirty, and her children were often sick with malaria from mosquitoes that bred in the nearby lakes. For the first time in her life, Stanton fully understood the plight of the isolated home-maker whose life revolved solely around keeping a house and raising children. "It seemed," she later wrote in her autobiography, "as if all the elements had conspired to impel me to some onward step. I could not see what to do or where to begin."

In this "tempest-tossed condition of mind," as she described herself in her autobiography, she went to visit Lucretia Mott in Waterloo. Joining Stanton and Mott that day were three other women: Martha Wright, Jane Hunt, and Mary Ann McClintock. As they sat around a table drinking tea, Stanton poured out "the torrent of my long-accumulating discontent, with such vehemence and indignation that I stirred myself, as well as the rest of the party, to do and dare anything."

What Stanton and the others dared to do was to organize a women's rights convention, which, they declared in an announcement in the local newspaper, would be devoted to the question of, "the social, civil, and religious condition and rights of women." That convention became known as the Seneca Falls Convention, and it set into motion the organized American women's rights movement.

"Tempest-tossed" and wholly devoted to the cause of women, Elizabeth Cady Stanton would soon stand at the very center of that movement, as its leader and, occasionally, as an opponent of other women's rights advocates who were not visionary or bold enough for her satisfaction. As she sat with the other four women on that momentous July 11, planning the Seneca Falls Convention, she had crossed a divide—from being a politician's wife and an occasional reformer herself to a warrior for female emancipation. The aftershocks of her actions continue to reverberate to this day.

*To the mischievous Elizabeth Cady, Johnstown, New York, was a somber place to grow up, but the
Cady house, above, provided her and her sisters with some amusements such as playing in the attic.
The girls also loved to roam the forests surrounding Johnstown and wade in the Cayadutta River,
despite their parents' prohibition.*

"I Taxed
Every Power"

In 1815, the year that Elizabeth Cady was born, Johnstown, New York, was a thriving town of about 1,000 citizens located 40 miles northwest of Albany, the state capital. Bound by the Cayadutta River to the north, Johnstown overlooked the sprawling Mohawk Valley, a region steeped in history and natural beauty. In autumn, the hillsides and valleys surrounding Johnstown were ablaze in fiery hues of scarlet, orange, and yellow. In winter, the entire area was blanketed in white, and young Elizabeth Cady and her sisters happily played in the snow.

Beyond Johnstown lay a young nation flush with confidence from fighting a much more powerful Great Britain to a draw in the War of 1812. No longer would the former mother country try to regain power over the nation that had won its independence three decades earlier. The outcome of the war was decisive: it helped to transform America into a more mature and independent country, with a greater sense of national unity.

In the early part of the 19th century, the landscape of America was rapidly changing from a loosely knit patchwork of small farms and villages to an interconnected web of bustling towns and commercial centers. By the 1790s, river currents had been harnessed to power factories. The water-powered cotton gin, a machine that processed cotton quickly and efficiently, had been invented in 1793, and it stimulated Southern farmers to expand the cultivation of cotton. This in turn spread the brutal system of slavery westward across the South.

In this changing social and economic landscape, Americans found their private lives changing as well. As the growing nation relied more on factories to produce its goods, many women no longer had to make all the products that their families consumed. They no longer wove the cloth for their families' apparel or made candles, soap, or any of the other goods that their families needed. Some women, especially young, single women, worked in the factories that made these goods, while other women continued to work at home, sewing for their families as well as for manufacturers who paid them by the piece.

As the economy changed and grew, people's perceptions of the social and economic roles that men and women should play also changed. Popular books and magazines and religious and intellectual leaders increasingly assigned separate roles to men and women: the active world of business and politics for men, and the more peaceful and private sphere of the home and family for women. Men were to be the breadwinners and political leaders, and women the loving, nurturing wives and mothers who willingly deferred to their husbands' authority.

Into this mannered world Elizabeth Cady was born on November 12, 1815. She came from a long and distinguished pedigree, the kind of traditional, established family that vigorously endorsed such distinct roles for women and men. Her mother, Margaret Livingston, was related by blood to some of the oldest and wealthiest families in New York State. Margaret Livingston's father, James Livingston, had commanded a regiment during the Revolutionary War and

Elizabeth Cady's mother, Margaret Livingston Cady, came from an upper-class lineage that included a Revolutionary War hero. Stanton later described her as "queenly," a testament to her stern and rather aloof nature.

had prevented Benedict Arnold, a traitor to the Revolution, from aiding the British. After the war, Livingston served on the first board of regents of New York's state university and in the state assembly.

Margaret Livingston Cady was a formidable woman. Standing nearly six feet tall, she was quiet and dignified, but she wielded considerable power at home and in Johnstown. She stood up to her equally strong-willed husband by refusing to move to a country estate far away from friends in town and by defying his ban on rocking chairs in their home. In her church, she insisted that female parishioners be allowed to vote for a new minister—an unusual step in a society in which women had little social or legal power. More important, despite her husband's stern opposition, she later supported abolition—the movement to end slavery—and women's rights. But central to her strong and principled nature was a severity that allowed little room for affection. Fear rather than love ruled the Cady household, and Elizabeth seldom heard praise from her mother's lips.

Elizabeth's father, Daniel Cady, was a self-made lawyer and landowner. Born into a farming family and apprenticed to a shoemaker, he became a schoolteacher after losing the sight in one eye in a cobbling accident. He went on to study law and later counted among his clients the business partner of wealthy financier and merchant John Jacob Astor. While advising his clients on real estate investments, Cady shrewdly purchased land for himself throughout New York State. He served in the New York State legislature and was elected to Congress in 1814, a year before Elizabeth was born. Roundly defeated in 1816, he returned to Johnstown to practice law and later moved up the judicial ranks to the position of associate justice of the New York State Supreme Court for the 4th District.

Unlike his wife, Cady was short, but he was equally reserved by nature. Deeply religious, he held conservative social and political views. In her autobiography, Elizabeth described her father as a "man of firm character and unimpeachable integrity, and yet sensitive and modest to a painful degree." Though he was gentle, he conducted himself with such reserve that "as children, we regarded him with fear rather than affection."

Elizabeth was the fourth daughter and eighth child in the Cady household. Her mother bore five sons, but four of them died in childhood. Another daughter followed two years after Elizabeth was born, and two years later, in 1819, yet another daughter was born—a profound disappointment in a society that looked to its sons to preserve the family's name and property holdings. Early on, Elizabeth learned that her family and community favored boys over girls.

Plump and fair-skinned, with rosy cheeks, dark brown hair, and shining blue eyes, Elizabeth was a precocious little

Daniel Cady came from humble beginnings and rose to prominence as a New York State judge. From her father, Stanton acquired much of the legal scholarship that helped shape her rhetoric and gave power to her arguments for women's rights.

girl who chafed at wearing itchy starched ruffles around her neck and who had trouble abiding by the strict rules at home and at school. One day, she asked her nurse, "Why [is it] that everything we like to do is a sin, and that everything we dislike is commanded by God or someone on earth?"

The Cady family attended the Scotch Presbyterian church, a denomination that adhered to traditional beliefs in the depravity of the human soul and in predestination—a belief that people had little or no control over their destiny and that God had already predetermined their deliverance to heaven or hell. For young Elizabeth, religious worship brought not joy and spiritual solace but terrifying visions of a

15

strange, mysterious world beyond the tomb. At funerals and Sunday services, the message imparted by the preacher was one of doom.

To make matters worse, being in church was intensely uncomfortable. The church was bare of ornament, and the service, in keeping with the Presbyterians' severe disdain for anything frivolous or uplifting, included neither an organ nor a choir; only a lone singer intoned line after line of the Psalms. Not even a furnace was available to provide heat. In the frigid depths of winter, Elizabeth and her family trudged through the snow, foot-stoves in hand to keep their feet from freezing in the "Lord's House." In the cold, bare church, they sat huddled for hours on hard wooden benches, chilled to the bone. Above them towered the preacher, who stood in an octagonal box, somberly warning them about their spiritual fate. To show any sign of fatigue or restlessness was to abandon one's soul to the devil.

But life in Johnstown was not entirely dreary. At home and around the village, Elizabeth and her sisters discovered new and different ways to have fun and get into mischief. Their house—an imposing two-story structure with tall windows and a hallway running down the center—had plenty of rooms to explore. Elizabeth's favorite parts of the house were the cellar and the attic. In wintertime the Cadys stored barrels of apples, vegetables, salted meats, cider, and butter in the cellar. The attic also held food stores, along with special treats such as barrels of hickory nuts, a long shelf that held cakes of maple syrup and dried herbs, and spinning wheels and old clothes. The girls loved to rummage in the attic and played blindman's buff in the cellar.

On warm summer evenings, Elizabeth and her sisters managed to squeeze through the bars in front of the windows of their second-story bedroom. Two of the windows opened onto a gently slanting roof over a veranda. There they sat, happily gazing up at the sky at the moon and the stars, breathing in the fragrant, balmy night air.

Johnstown itself provided the girls with a variety of amusements and curiosities. Many distinguished lawyers argued cases at the courthouse and then joined the Cadys for dinner. Elizabeth listened attentively to the spirited legal discussions around her family's dinner table. She also visited the courthouse and the jail and was keenly moved by the plight of the prisoners and by the rough jailhouse conditions. Johnstown was a small place, but for Elizabeth it was a window to a larger world of swirling legal and political ferment.

Early on, Elizabeth encountered the twin evils of racial and sexual prejudice. Slavery was not abolished in New York State until 1827, when Elizabeth was 12. So it is possible that the three black servants whom she recalled so fondly in later years—Abraham, Peter, and Jacob—were actually slaves. On Christmas morning, the Cady daughters usually accompanied Peter to services at the Episcopalian church. They sat with him in the back by the door, in the "Negro pew." He had to wait until all of the white worshipers had taken communion before he was allowed to go up to the altar.

Elizabeth's first encounter with laws that treated women unequally came within her own home. Because her father's law office adjoined the house, she spent much time there reading his books and listening to his discussions with clients who sought legal advice. Some of these clients were women who had been widowed and had no legal claim to their husbands' property. In New York State, and indeed throughout most of the country, women had no legal identity after they were married. They could not own property—including their own wages if they worked—or sign contracts. Nor could they claim guardianship of their children in divorce proceedings or testify against their husbands in court. Many states even granted husbands the right to inflict corporal punishment on their wives and specified the instrument they could use.

One woman's plight, in particular, aroused Elizabeth's indignation. On her husband's death, Flora Campbell, a family servant, sought to reclaim a farm that she had purchased with her own money and that her husband had willed to an irresponsible and uncaring son. Elizabeth's father sadly explained that he was powerless to help her, because the property now legally belonged to her son. For the first time, Elizabeth understood that laws could hurt as well as protect people, and that if such laws remained in force women would never be treated equally.

Shortly before Elizabeth turned 11, a tragic turn of events overtook the Cady household. Twenty-year-old Eleazer, the only Cady son, became seriously ill. Elizabeth's father was devastated; Eleazer was "the very apple of my father's eye," Elizabeth recalled in her autobiography—the one and only son on whom Judge Cady pinned such high hopes and ambitious plans for the future. Elizabeth watched her father keep a vigil by his son's bedside, leaving only to pace the hall in despair. When Eleazer died, the entire household was wreathed in mourning.

To please her father and help him overcome his grief, Elizabeth decided that she would try to be just like Eleazer. She set herself the task of excelling at the skills that a son was expected to master. She became an agile horseback rider and undertook the study of Greek. "I thought that the chief thing to be done in order to equal boys was to be learned and courageous," she explained later. She enlisted the assistance of the Cadys' pastor and neighbor, Reverend Hosack, to teach her Greek, and quickly memorized the Greek alphabet, astonishing the preacher.

No less impressive than Elizabeth's mastery of Greek was her skill and speed at learning how to ride horseback. "I taxed every power," she recalled later in her autobiography, "hoping some day to hear my father say, 'Well, a girl is as good as a boy, after all.'" But Judge Cady pined for his lost son and barely noticed Elizabeth.

Although Reverend Hosack espoused traditional religious ideas, he respected Elizabeth's intellectual abilities and treated her with affection and respect—qualities sorely lacking in her relationship with her stern and remote parents. She helped Reverend Hosack in his garden, and he often let her drive him on his rounds while he read aloud from *Blackwell's Magazine* or *The Edinburgh Review,* stopping to explain complex ideas to her.

Shortly after her brother's death, Elizabeth stopped attending a small dame school—a school taught by a woman in her own home—and entered Johnstown Academy. Although the school was coed, Elizabeth was the only girl in the upper-level Latin, Greek, and mathematics classes. Most of her fellow students in these classes were older than she, but the quick-minded Elizabeth excelled. Three years in a row, she placed second in her Greek class. One year, she even received a prize and eagerly ran home to show it to her father. She rushed into his office and proudly displayed her prize, a Greek New Testament. She waited in eager anticipation for words of praise. But he merely kissed her on the forehead and sighed, "Ah, you should have been a boy!" Elizabeth was crushed.

Edward Bayard, the husband of Tryphena Cady, treated Elizabeth with special care. He gave her the loving attention that her own father did not, took Elizabeth and her friends hiking and horseback riding, and introduced her to new books and ideas.

In 1827, the mood of the Cady household lightened considerably when Edward Bayard, a classmate of Eleazer's at Union College, married Elizabeth's older sister Tryphena and came to live with the Cadys. Bayard, originally from Wilmington, Delaware, was studying law with Judge Cady. Elizabeth was immediately drawn to the tall, handsome young man, and he, in turn, became like the family's son and brother. Judge Cady was frequently away from home on legal business and Mrs. Cady, worn out and grieving, had simply withdrawn. Edward and Tryphena quickly assumed responsibility for Elizabeth and her two younger sisters.

Like substitute parents, they brought laughter and loving attention into the household. They selected the girls' clothing, books, and entertainment and supervised their progress at school.

The new arrangement clearly suited Elizabeth. Although Tryphena valiantly attempted to practice her mother's strict discipline, Edward cheerfully undermined her by acting more as the girls' confidant and affectionate older brother than as a stern parent. In her autobiography, Elizabeth recalled that with Edward "came an era of picnics, birthday parties, and endless amusements." Edward and his brother, Henry, who was also studying with Judge Cady, lavished the girls with gifts, from books and pictures to ponies and musical instruments, and turned schoolwork into a game. Like Reverend Hosack, Edward respected Elizabeth's sharp mind and eagerly discussed complex ideas such as the law with her.

Few other people in Johnstown shared Edward Bayard's or Reverend Hosack's enlightened ideas about educating young women. In 1831, 16-year-old Elizabeth and her classmates graduated from Johnstown Academy. The boys in her class prepared to continue their education at Union College in Schenectady, New York, where her brother Eleazer had gone. Elizabeth's father brushed aside all notions of additional education for her. Instead, he suggested that she accompany him out of town on judicial business and enjoy the balls and dinners. Elizabeth gamely tried each of these activities, but she yearned for more education.

Once again Edward Bayard came to her rescue. He persuaded Elizabeth's parents to send her to Troy Female Seminary in Troy, New York. Troy was one of several female academies in the Northeast that offered a rigorous academic education to young women. These seminaries were a form of college for young women, because no colleges at the time accepted women. But Troy was unique. Founded by Emma Hart Willard in 1821, it was the first seminary to supplement the traditional curriculum for women—music,

French, and needlepoint—with a demanding academic course of study.

Willard was a maverick, an ardent advocate of women's education at a time when most people questioned why women needed to learn more than the household arts. Although she argued that her school would better prepare women for marriage and motherhood—and therefore help to strengthen the moral fiber of the new nation—she also claimed that educating women would help meet the nation's growing demand for teachers. Consequently, Troy Female Seminary offered training in both domestic arts and academic subjects, including such science and math classes as trigonometry, astronomy, chemistry, botany, mineralogy, and physiology, more advanced than those offered in many men's colleges. Though Willard called her school a "female seminary," she strove to make it the academic equal of the best men's colleges in the nation.

In the winter of 1831, Elizabeth boarded a train for the journey to Troy. The frigid temperature outside matched her chilly state of mind. She felt hopeless: here she was, the intellectual equal of the best male students at Johnstown Academy, forced to settle for what she scorned as a girls' finishing school. But with every mile the train covered, Elizabeth Cady drew closer to a new world, a place to test her skills, her knowledge, and her dreams away from the stern gaze of her family.

CHAPTER

"A NEW INSPIRATION IN LIFE"

Elizabeth Cady began classes at Troy Female Seminary on January 2, 1831. The first term was already half over, but the quick-minded Elizabeth soon caught up academically with her classmates. Although she later claimed in her auto-biography that she had already studied everything that was taught at Troy, except French, music, and dancing—"so I devoted myself to these accomplishments"—her school records show that she took algebra, Greek, and music during her first term and studied logic, botany, writing, geometry, and modern history in the second term.

The rectangular three-story brick building lay in the center of Troy, a prosperous community just across the Hudson River from Albany. By 1831, the seminary boasted an enrollment of more than 100 students who boarded there, including Elizabeth, and 200 day students. Although grateful to be receiving a college education, Elizabeth missed the stimulating companionship of male students and abhorred the "pretensions and petty jealousies" of the other girls. But she admired and respected Emma Willard, the school's director. Willard continued to expand the school's path-breaking curriculum while Elizabeth was there.

Perhaps her most innovative course offering was physiology; Willard had no patience with popular beliefs that women were too delicate to learn about the human body. Her students memorized the names and functions of all the human organs.

Gradually Elizabeth became more comfortable with her new surroundings. As she recalled in her autobiography, "The large house, the society of so many girls, the walks about the city, the novelty of everything made the new life more enjoyable than I had anticipated." But there was one aspect of her new life that

Elizabeth Cady at 20 was pretty and vivacious. She had a great fondness for practical jokes and loved nothing more than a good party.

Elizabeth did not enjoy, because it aroused old fears about the devil and her own religious shortcomings. Troy was right in the path of the Second Great Awakening, an intense religious movement that swept through the towns and villages along the Erie Canal in upstate New York. Indeed, there were so many intense, dramatic revivals throughout this region that people began to call it the "burned over district." Unlike in earlier religious movements, more women than men converted, and they fervently responded to preachers' urgings to uphold moral and religious values in a society increasingly devoted to acquiring wealth and material objects.

In contrast with the stern Scotch Presbyterian faith that Elizabeth's family adhered to, the Second Great Awakening was more democratic in spirit and encouraged an outpouring of expression from preachers as well as their audiences, who writhed and moaned to the preacher's thunderous words. When some of her classmates went to the revival meetings in Troy, Elizabeth tagged along and quickly fell under the spell of the preacher's fervor.

At these revival meetings, Charles Grandison Finney, a preacher well known for his fire-and-brimstone style, ranted about the devil and the long procession of sinners plunging into the flaming depths of Hell. He glared at his listners and waved his arms about like a windmill. At one meeting, he suddenly stopped and pointed his index finger. "There, do you not see them?" he insisted. Elizabeth was so startled that she jumped up and stared at where he was pointing.

Night after night, she lay awake in bed, haunted by his dreadful description of the fiery doom that lurked below. She could not sleep and was so distraught that she became ill. During a visit home, she woke her father up almost every night to pray for her and save her from hell. Judge Cady, alarmed by his daughter's anguish, forbade Elizabeth from attending any more revivals.

He also planned a trip to Niagara Falls to restore Elizabeth's confidence. In June 1831, she, her father, and Tryphena and Edward Bayard embarked on a six-week vacation. Gradually, under Bayard's gentle, good-humored tutelage, Elizabeth overcame her religious fears and regained her cheerful outlook on life. Later, on long winter evenings, with a fire blazing in the hearth, Bayard introduced her to the poetry of Sir Walter Scott and the novels of James Fenimore Cooper and Charles Dickens. He hoped that these great works of literature would help Elizabeth to shed her remaining religious superstitions.

In 1833, Elizabeth graduated from Troy Female Seminary and returned to Johnstown. She was now 18, the age when many young women were married, but she had no prospects and she did not seem to care. She embarked upon the leisurely, genteel life of an upper-class young woman who was not forced to work.

Petite and vivacious, with curly brown hair, sparkling eyes, and a winning smile, Elizabeth Cady enjoyed an active social life—a round of parties, dances, hayrides, horse races, and visits to relatives, especially to the home of her older cousin Gerrit Smith in Peterboro, New York.

At Gerrit Smith's house, Cady also met abolitionists and important social reformers, politicians, and even runaway slaves. She participated in stimulating dinnertime debates about the antislavery cause and temperance, the movement to ban the consumption of alcohol. Smith, a man of considerable wealth, possessed a keen interest in social reform and used his wealth to support the causes dear to him. He advocated prison reform, less confining clothing for women, an end to capital punishment, and a ban on alcohol. He was also an ardent abolitionist who advocated the immediate end to slavery and served as the president of the New York chapter of the American Anti-Slavery Society from 1836 to 1839.

At his house, Elizabeth Cady also came into contact with intriguing new ideas and activists eager to improve all aspects of American life. For many years, female benevolent societies had been distributing Bible tracts, assisting the ill and destitute, and helping widows and children. But now, in the 1830s, these and other groups found new and more effective ways to accomplish their reform goals. Women, in particular, developed important organizational and leadership skills in their reform groups. They learned how to draft their own constitutions and bylaws, elect officers, organize meetings, manage money, and write and publish progress reports. They also learned how to circulate petitions and testify before courts and state legislative committees.

As early as the 1820s, women in the North had joined male-led organizations to end slavery. Soon they formed their own groups. These societies channeled their female members' discontent with the limited domestic scope of their lives and inspired them to feel they were contributing to the betterment of their communities. By 1837, 77 out of 1,000 antislavery societies were exclusively female.

Despite widespread public disapproval of abolition, and especially of women's participation in the abolition movement, female abolitionists persevered in their work. At their meetings, they faced down hostile mobs and defied the opposition of community leaders such as ministers and newspaper editors. They circulated petitions to grant citizenship to blacks in their communities, raised funds to pay for legal counsel or the freedom of runaway slaves, worked with the Underground Railroad, and spoke in public.

Antislavery women were greatly influenced by the ideas of William Lloyd Garrison, the most famous and also most reviled leader of the abolition movement. Garrison, who lived in Boston and edited an antislavery newspaper, *The Liberator,* regarded blacks and whites as equal human beings who were entitled to the same rights and privileges. Antislavery women applied this principle to men and women. They challenged a social order in which men held all social and political power by insisting that women, as human beings, were the equals of men and therefore deserved equal rights. Elizabeth Cady attended antislavery conventions where Garrison, Frederick Douglass, a former slave and celebrated orator, and the Quaker reformer Lucretia Mott spoke. She relished the many opportunities to argue, debate, and think for herself, and she felt, as she later recalled in her autobiography, "a new inspiration in life."

Besides famous reformers, Elizabeth Cady met one other significant person at Gerrit Smith's home—her future husband, Henry Stanton. Like Edward Bayard, he was 10 years older than Cady, and he shared Gerrit Smith's passionate commitment to abolition. Indeed, Henry Stanton was a well-known abolitionist who lectured around the country. In October 1839, she heard him lecture and was enthralled by his powerful oration. Perhaps, too, she was drawn to his

Gerrit Smith had a profound influence on his young cousin Elizabeth Cady. At his house in Peterboro, New York, which was a stop on the Underground Railroad, she met abolitionists, temperance activists, and other dedicated social reformers.

dignified manner and striking good looks. He had gentle, deep-set eyes and strong, chiseled features framed by a full mustache and sideburns. Soon after they met, Cady and Stanton went horseback riding. As they rode along country paths, they discovered a quiet pleasure in each other's company. As they walked their horses through a detour in a grove of trees, Henry Stanton "laid his hand on the horn of the saddle and, to my surprise," she recalled in her autobiography, he proposed marriage. She accepted on the spot.

Cady's elation soon turned to anguish when Gerrit Smith pointed out to her that her father would never consent to a marriage with Stanton. Gerrit reminded her that not only was Stanton an abolitionist—a vocation that Judge Cady and most other conservative men of wealth loathed—but, because he was not wealthy, he had no prospects for supporting Cady.

At Smith's suggestion, Cady wrote her father to break the news of her engagement from afar, hoping that his anger would vanish by the time she returned home. But, as Smith had predicted, when she returned to Johnstown she found that Judge Cady was fiercely opposed to her marrying Henry Stanton. Her father warned her that Stanton could not support her, and he proceeded to remind her of the status of married women in New York State—that wives had no legal right to own or inherit property in their own names, keep their earnings, sign contracts, initiate lawsuits, claim more than one-third of their husbands' estates, or secure custody or control of their own children.

What should have been a season of joy and excitement for Cady became, as she later said in her autobiography, a period of "doubt and conflict...doubt as to the wisdom of changing a girlhood

This sketch of Henry Stanton was made about the time that he met Elizabeth Cady at Gerrit Smith's house after speaking at a nearby antislavery meeting. Stanton had planned to enter the ministry, but in 1835 he began a career as an abolitionist.

of freedom and enjoyment for I knew not what, and conflict because the step I proposed was in opposition to the wishes of all my family."

Valiantly Stanton tried to reassure her of his abiding love. On New Year's Day 1840, he wrote to her, "Among [all your friends] thou shalt not find one who loves thee more devotedly, or would do more to render this & all thy future years 'happy,' than him whose hand traces these lines."

But Stanton's pleas were no match for the disapproval of Cady's father. Sometime in January or February 1840, she broke off their engagement, deciding that she had been "too hasty." As she explained in a letter to Ann Fitzhugh Smith, Gerrit Smith's wife, "We are still friends & correspond as before & perhaps when the storm blows over we may be dearer friends than now."

Soon, however, something changed her mind: Henry Stanton was about to sail to Europe for several months to attend the World's Anti-Slavery Convention as a delegate of the newly formed American and Foreign Anti-Slavery Society. Stanton, Gerrit Smith, and several other leaders had broken off from the main emancipation group led by William Lloyd Garrison. In April 1840, they established their own political party—the Liberty party—and nominated James G. Birney, a former slave owner who had become an abolitionist, as a Presidential candidate. Garrison and his followers did not support direct political action to free slaves, preferring instead to rely on moral persuasion. The two groups also differed on the role of women within the abolition movement. Garrison favored women voting, holding office, and serving as delegates. Because they did not want to alienate male voters, Stanton's group did not support female participation within their group.

When Cady learned that Henry would be on another continent for eight months, she insisted that they get married before he left. They decided to marry quickly and quietly, and rejected an elaborate ceremony. On May 1, 1840, they were married in the presence of a few friends. She wore a simple white evening dress. The Reverend Hugh Maire, minister of her family's church, performed the ceremony. Cady chose to keep her surname and added "Stanton"; her full name was now Elizabeth Cady Stanton. She also insisted that Reverend Maire omit the word "obey" from her marriage vows. As she explained in her autobiography, "I obstinately refused to obey one with whom I supposed I was entering into an equal relation."

On their way to London, the newlyweds paid a visit to Belleville, New Jersey, at the home of Henry Stanton's best friend, Theodore Weld; his wife, Angelina; and Sarah Grimké, Angelina's sister. Sarah and Angelina Grimké had earlier played a courageous and important role in the abolition movement. The daughters of a Charleston, South Carolina, slave owner, they had witnessed first-hand the horrors of slavery and detested the system. In 1821, Sarah joined the Quaker faith, which opposed slavery, and moved to Philadelphia, an important hub of the Quaker community. Angelina soon followed Sarah's example and also converted to Quakerism. She moved to Philadelphia and joined the Female Anti-Slavery Society. Both women became ardent abolitionists who lectured on the evils of slavery.

Finally, on May 12, 1840, Henry and Elizabeth Cady Stanton boarded the ship *Montreal* for their voyage to London. As the New York City skyline receded behind them, Elizabeth Cady Stanton eagerly anticipated the adventures that awaited her—the opportunity to participate in a momentous international gathering on the most burning issue of the day, to explore a continent she had never visited before, and to share her life with a man who adored her. Life seemed truly rich and bountiful.

This painting of the 1840 World's Anti-Slavery Convention in London records the segregation of the women delegates. The women were seated behind the men and were denied the opportunity to speak. Henry Stanton is the man with sideburns seated in the front row in the second seat from the right.

"A New Born Sense of Dignity and Freedom"

The novelty of ship life wore thin after about a week, and Stanton began to feel restless and eager for land. Her fellow passengers were no help in breaking the monotony of the voyage. "They were all stolid, middle-class English people," she recalled in her autobiography, traveling from various parts of the world to visit their native land. Nor was James Birney, the Stantons' fellow delegate to the World's Anti-Slavery Convention, any livelier. "He kept to himself like a clam in his shell all the time," Stanton wrote to the Grimké sisters.

One day, the captain, a "jolly fellow" who delighted in telling Stanton about his adventurous sailor's life, dared her to be hoisted to the top of the mast in a chair while all the other passengers were dining. Never one to turn down a dare, Stanton gleefully had herself hoisted up. Birney, of course, was horrified—a few nights later, after a game of chess, he admonished her for her unladylike behavior. But Stanton did not spend all her time aboard ship in frivolous pursuits. She devoted much of her days to reading and educating herself about the abolition movement back home.

The *Montreal* reached England on May 31, and the Stantons and Birney disembarked near Exeter. The next day, they set out for London. On first sight, as she later recalled, Stanton thought their lodging house on Queen Street, in the East End of London near the River Thames, was the "gloomiest abode I had ever seen." But the arrival of female delegates from Boston and Philadelphia quickly enlivened the dour place. Stanton eagerly introduced herself to several female abolitionists, including Ann Green Phillips, who was newly married to the reformer Wendell Phillips and was also on her wedding trip, and Lucretia Mott, the highly respected Quaker leader from Philadelphia. Stanton was instantly drawn to Mott, who was her elder by 22 years and who had already distinguished herself as a dedicated reformer and independent thinker.

Mott's petite stature and serene countenance, usually framed by a simple bonnet, masked a formidable woman with a keen, searching intellect and a backbone of iron. In her autobiography, Stanton said of her, "The amount of will force and intelligent power in her small body was enough to direct the universe." A Quaker minister (the Quakers were unusual for that time in that they allowed women to be ministers), Mott was a passionate believer in the equality of men and women. She gradually rejected traditional forms of Quaker thought and worship and came to believe in the presence of an inner spirit, or light, in each person. This inner spirit embodied the divine and guided people toward making moral and humane choices.

As Mott heeded her inner spirit, her opposition to slavery grew even more intense. In 1833, she helped to organize the Philadelphia Female Antislavery Society, and also joined

Lucretia Mott, a highly respected Quaker reformer and abolitionist, was also an ardent champion of women's social and political equality. Stanton called her a "peerless woman."

the American Anti-Slavery Society when it was formed that same year. Her support for William Lloyd Garrison's radical demand for immediate emancipation of all American slaves aroused the disapproval of more conservative Quakers. But Mott, accustomed to facing down vicious opponents of abolition, was thoroughly unmoved by their condemnation.

Stanton could not stay away from her. "Wherever our party went," she later wrote Mott's son, "I took possession of Lucretia, much to Henry's vexation." To Elizabeth Cady Stanton, Mott was "an entire new revelation of womanhood." Years later, Stanton recalled in her autobiography, "I sought every opportunity to be at her side, and continually plied her with questions."

Mott explained to Stanton the ideas and disputes among Quakers regarding the inner light, and the two women had many probing discussions about the connection between religion and reform. Accustomed to the cramped Scotch Presbyterian tradition, which tolerated no questioning of Scripture, Stanton was astonished by Mott's independent religious thinking. "When I first heard from her lips that I had the same right to think for myself...and the same right to be guided by my own convictions, I felt a new born sense of dignity and freedom."

The World's Anti-Slavery Convention opened on June 12, 1840, in Freemason's Hall in London. Four hundred delegates filled the large hall, hoping to exchange ideas on the most effective way to end slavery and help newly freed blacks. But almost immediately, another question occupied delegates—whether to recognize the American women, including Lucretia Mott, as official delegates or relegate them to the visitors' gallery, where they could watch but not participate in the proceedings. The convention erupted in heated dispute. Wendell Phillips proposed recognizing all delegates with credentials from any antislavery society, regardless of sex. But the Stantons' shipmate James Birney and others opposed the motion. Several English clergymen insisted that allowing the women to participate would be "promiscuous" and even sacrilegious. After all, they argued, the Bible proclaimed women to be the weaker sex and therefore subject to men's authority. Henry Stanton also spoke. Although he supported Phillips's motion, he is thought to have cast his vote with the anti-Garrisons who opposed women's participation.

Throughout all the debate and speech making, the women were cordoned off on one side of the hall, unable to speak in their own behalf. Humiliated, Stanton sat there fuming at the "shallow reasoning" and "comical pose and gestures" of the opponents of women's participation. She could not believe that these "narrow-minded bigots, pretending to be teachers and leaders of men" would dare silence the likes of Lucretia Mott.

Finally the male delegates voted and roundly defeated Phillips's motion. The women were barred from participating as delegates in the convention, even though many of them had traveled long distances for precisely that reason and were dedicated members of their own antislavery groups. All they could do was silently watch their male comrades. When Garrison, who arrived later, learned of this injustice, he promptly went and sat with the women to protest the convention's efforts to silence them. From London he wrote his wife, "Mrs. Stanton is a fearless woman and goes for women's rights with all her soul."

When the convention adjourned for that day, Stanton and Mott walked out together. As they strode back to the lodging house, "arm in arm, commenting on the incidents of the day," recalled Stanton in her autobiography, "we resolved to hold a convention as soon as we returned home, and form a society to advocate the rights of women."

Henry and Elizabeth Cady Stanton spent a month in London, exploring every corner of the city, from the majestic Westminster Abbey to the forbidding Tower of London. They toured museums and attended both sessions of Parliament.

From London, they journeyed out to the rest of England. To finance their travels, Henry had arranged to lecture on American abolition and write a series of articles for two American journals. The lecture tour gave Elizabeth Stanton an opportunity to meet some of England's leading thinkers and reformers and take in the historical sites and breathtaking scenery of the English countryside.

Stanton was heartened to find so many friends of abolition in England. Only seven years before, in 1833, Britain had abolished slavery throughout its empire. But in the United States, Southern planters and politicians clung fiercely to the system of bondage. They had already passed laws forbidding slaves to learn how to read or write, fearing they would use these skills to plan a rebellion, and, to preserve their way of life, they urged the expansion of slavery into new territories opening for settlement.

In the United States, speaking out against slavery took courage, and women were not exempt from the wrath of anti-abolitionists. In 1835, when the Boston Female Anti-Slavery Society sponsored an interracial meeting, mobs went wild at the prospect of black and white women associating together. As angry protestors surrounded the hall, shouting obscenities, Maria Weston Chapman, the leader of the society, calmly conducted the meeting and rejected any suggestions of canceling it. "If this is the last bulwark of freedom," she declared, "we might as well die here." After the meeting, William Lloyd Garrison tried to sneak out the back, but the mob caught him and dragged him through town by the end of a rope. Back at the meeting hall, the women arranged themselves in pairs, one black woman and one white, and resolutely walked through the jeering crowd.

At home, Stanton had read about such frightening incidents, but in England she was delighted to find overwhelming support for abolition. Later, she and Henry traveled to France, Scotland, and Ireland. Stanton was appalled by the poverty she saw in Ireland. Beggars followed them everywhere—in

THE LIBERATOR
COMMENCED JANUARY 1st 1831.

W.L.G.

"I am in earnest! I will not equivocate — I will not excuse! I will not retreat a single inch — And *I WILL BE HEARD!*"

This banner shows the masthead of The Liberator, *the antislavery newspaper edited by William Lloyd Garrison. Stanton was greatly influenced by Garrison's uncompromising views on human equality and natural rights.*

the street and on the highways, stalking them outside their lodgings and surrounding their carriages wherever they stopped. For the first time, she witnessed a huge gap between rich and poor and began to ponder how this social and economic inequality could be corrected.

In December 1840, the Stantons boarded the Cunard steamer *Sirius* in Liverpool, England, for the journey home. On returning to Johnstown, Stanton found that her father's opposition to her marriage had somehow vanished. Now she and Henry had to decide where to live. After consulting with Judge Cady, Henry Stanton decided to study law with him, and his young wife happily consented to live in her parents' house. She spent carefree days with her younger sisters, who were still living at home, and read intensively in law, history, and political science.

Stanton corresponded regularly with Lucretia Mott and other women she had met in London. With a neighbor in Johnstown, she taught a Sunday school class to black children. When some prejudiced church members locked the children out of the church during a religious festival, Stanton and the other teacher indignantly took them to the Cady home for their own celebration.

Although she did not devote much time to antislavery activities, Stanton remained a dedicated abolitionist. She avidly read and spoke privately about the abolition movement and women's rights, but made few actual attempts to promote either cause. She was not a member of any abolition organizations, and she had not yet taken up the cause of women's rights with great fervor.

These were formative years in her intellectual and political growth. Though she disagreed with her husband's opposition to Garrison—and with the efforts of his competing organization, the American and Foreign Anti-Slavery Society, to silence women's participation—she agreed with the group's goals to create a new political party and run its own Presidential candidate. As she wrote to her friend Elizabeth Pease in February 1842, "As I am not yet fully converted to the doctrine of no human government, I am in favour of political action.... So long as we are to be governed by human laws, I should be unwilling to have the making & administering of those laws left entirely to the selfish & unprincipled part of the community, which would be the case should all our honest men refuse to mingle in political affairs." Stanton was beginning to understand that political questions required political action—a lesson that she would soon put into practice for women's rights.

On March 2, 1842, Stanton gave birth to her first child, Daniel Cady Stanton, called Neil for short. Stanton had full

Sarah Grimké wrote and published this series of letters a full decade before the Seneca Falls Convention. "I ask no favors for my sex," she declared in the letters. "All I ask of our brethren is that they will take their feet from off our necks and permit us to stand upright on the ground which God has deigned us to occupy."

LETTERS

ON THE

EQUALITY OF THE SEXES,

AND THE

CONDITION OF WOMAN.

ADDRESSED TO

MARY S. PARKER,

PRESIDENT OF THE

Boston Female Anti-Slavery Society.

———

BOSTON:

PUBLISHED BY ISAAC KNAPP,

25, CORNHILL.

1838.

responsibility for her baby's care, because her husband was away during much of Neil's infancy, either traveling on antislavery business or staying in Boston, where he intended to practice law, to study for admission to the Massachusetts bar. Stanton had done extensive reading and thinking about proper infant care. She quickly rejected most traditional practices such as swaddling the baby tightly in blankets. Over the nurse's objections, she dressed Neil in comfortable loose gowns, opened the windows and curtains in his nursery to let in fresh air and sunlight, and insisted that the nurse refrain from singing mournful songs such as "Hark, from the tombs a doleful sound!"

Henry Stanton passed the bar on October 4, 1842, and Elizabeth Cady Stanton began shuttling back and forth between Boston and Albany, New York, where her father had secured a townhouse for his family. Although Henry joined a law firm, he spent almost as much time on politics. He was active in the newly formed Liberty party's Massachusetts campaign to win more seats in the state legislature, and in 1843 he served as chairman of the party's state central committee. His political activities helped to put more antislavery activists in office, but they did nothing to fill the family's coffers. He confessed to James Birney how concerned his wife was. "[She] feels very bad, and is sometimes quite gloomy with the apprehension that we shall not get through the coming year."

On March 15, 1844, Stanton gave birth to another son, Henry B. Stanton, at her father's townhouse in Albany, and Judge Cady gave his daughter and her growing family a generous gift—a house in Boston. With the help of two servants, Stanton eagerly took up housekeeping. She relished managing her own home. Even the tedious chore of doing laundry held a certain charm for her. The house had a balcony with a sweeping view of Boston, the harbor, and the surrounding countryside. Stanton loved to stand on the balcony and gaze out at the bustling city. Later she recalled in her autobiography, "There, on the upper piazza, I spent some of the happiest days of my life, enjoying, in turn, the beautiful outlook, my children, and my books."

Before her lay a city that considered itself the hub of the world, and it was indeed a magnet for interesting new ideas and people. Poets, philosophers, social reformers, and other celebrated thinkers and activists made their way to Boston, and Stanton met them all, from the poet John Greenleaf Whittier to the essayist and philosopher Ralph Waldo Emerson to Lydia Maria Child, Abby Kelly, and Maria Chapman, three dedicated antislavery activists. Stanton attended lectures, concerts, and theater performances, as well as antislavery, temperance, peace, and prison-reform conventions. She spent many stimulating and sociable evenings at William Garrison's home. There, she met Frederick Douglass, the former slave who was now an eloquent orator. He mesmerized Stanton with his dignity and powerful words.

During long visits to her parents' home in Johnstown throughout 1843 to 1845, Stanton also joined other women in circulating petitions to give married women in New York State greater control of their property. As early as 1836, advocates had lobbied for a bill that would grant married women possession of property they had inherited or acquired, but the bill failed to pass the state legislature. Now the time seemed ripe to renew efforts to get a bill passed, and Stanton, who supported the bill on principle and also to seek protection for her own inheritance, circulated petitions and lobbied members of the legislature. The bill eventually became law in 1848, the first legislation of its kind in the United States.

Amid this whirl of activity, Stanton found herself hungering for spiritual sustenance. In Boston, she began attending church services and lectures on theology. She was especially captivated by the ideas of Theodore Parker, a Unitarian minister who advocated abolition, temperance (a movement to ban the consumption of alcohol), and women's rights. Parker infused his religious ideas with a good dose of Transcendentalism, a new way of thinking that claimed to perceive the beauty and presence of God in the natural world and in every person. Transcendentalism celebrated nature and the individual's inborn spiritual connection to the natural world.

On September 18, 1845, Stanton gave birth to a third son, Gerrit Smith Stanton, named after her beloved cousin. Meanwhile, she was thriving in Boston. She loved her home and domestic life, and she was intoxicated by the tempestuous whirl of people and ideas. But Henry Stanton did not share her contentment. Although his law practice was flourishing, his political career was not. Eager to find better political opportunities elsewhere, he turned his sights to Seneca Falls, New York, where he thought he would find more support for his political positions. Henry was prophetic in thinking that Seneca Falls would offer new opportunities—not for him, however, but for his wife.

Stanton, who was a loving and permissive mother, was photographed with her second oldest son, Henry, around 1855. Of raising children, she said, "We must inspire them with confidence in themselves and show them how to do what they desire."

4

"WOMAN HERSELF MUST DO THIS WORK"

If Boston was the hub of the world, then Seneca Falls was a slender spoke. In the fall of 1847, when the Stantons moved there with their three young sons, Seneca Falls was a village of about 4,000 citizens with six churches, four hotels, and one academy. It also housed many small factories and mills, which produced cotton cloth, flour, paper, axes, leather, liquor, boats, window sashes, and water pumps. People and goods could be carried by rail or by ship along the Cayuga and Seneca Canal, which was connected to the Erie Canal, a major waterway for shipping and transportation.

Once again, Judge Cady gave the Stantons their home— a house and two acres—as well as a nearby farm. The two-story, L-shaped clapboard house with a roomy front porch occupied a corner lot of overgrown land on Washington Street, on the edge of town, and needed many repairs. Stanton hired carpenters, painters, paperhangers, and gardeners to spruce up the house and yard. She had a new kitchen and woodshed built, and the family moved in a few weeks later.

She and Henry named the house "Grassmere," after the poet William Wordsworth's home, which the Stantons had visited in England. But the house in Seneca Falls lacked the

cozy charm of its namesake. As in Boston, Henry was away a great deal. Stanton was left in charge of the house and family, a role that she took to naturally, but Seneca Falls had none of Boston's lively intellectual and cultural offerings. She felt lonely and isolated. Simply going downtown was a chore, because the roads were often muddy and there were hardly any sidewalks. To make matters worse, the swamps around Seneca Falls bred malaria, and the boys—already a handful at ages five, three, and two—were constantly sick with chills and fever, as were Stanton's servants.

When Stanton—along with Martha Wright, Jane Hunt, and Mary Ann McClintock—went to visit Lucretia Mott in nearby Waterloo on Tuesday, July 11, 1848, she was ready to revolt, but it is unlikely she would have done anything without the encouragement of the other women, especially Mott. Among the five women, Mott was the oldest at 54, and Stanton, 32, was the youngest. Except for Stanton, all the women were liberal Quakers whose religious beliefs included active participation in social reform. But only Mott had extensive experience as an organizer and public speaker. As Stanton later described them in her autobiography, they "were neither sour old maids, childless women, nor divorced wives, as the newspapers declared them to be." Instead, they had "souls large enough to feel the wrongs of others."

As their first order of business, they drafted an announcement that appeared in the afternoon edition of the *Seneca
County Courier* on July 14 to call a "Convention to discuss
the social, civil, and religious condition and rights of woman."
The convention was to take place on July 19 and 20 at the
Methodist Church in Seneca Falls—that gave them five days
to set the agenda and also to write a manifesto setting forth
their grievances.

At first they felt overwhelmed by the task of trying to
put into words the injustices that women suffered. As they
set about drafting the declaration, recalled Stanton in her
autobiography, they felt "as helpless and hopeless as if they
had been suddenly asked to construct a steam engine."
While the five women scribbled and argued, they consulted
the work of other women who had demanded an end to
sexual discrimination. As early as 1792, Mary Wollstonecraft,
a British novelist and essayist, had written a treatise entitled
A Vindication of the Rights of Woman, in which she laid out
the many ways that social custom and legal tradition prevented women from achieving full equality with men.
America's own Margaret Fuller, another advocate of women's
rights, had set forth her ideas on women's potential in the
book *Woman in the Nineteenth Century* in 1845. She rejected
any limitations on women's sphere of activities and urged
them to seek an education and work at whatever they
desired. "Let them be sea captains if they will," Fuller
declared in her book.

Sarah and Angelina Grimké had found their way to the
cause of women's rights through their antislavery work.
Both women were eloquent public speakers for the abolition movement. But when they encountered opposition
from some conservative New England clergymen, who did
not believe that women should speak in public, they rose up
in protest and defended the right of women to act as moral,
intelligent, and responsible beings. Sarah Grimké wrote a
series of letters on "The Equality of the Sexes and the

THE COURIER.

Semi-Weekly—Circulation One Thousand.

FRIDAY, AUGUST 4, 1848.

Women's Rights Convention.

A Convention to discuss the social, civil and religious condition and rights of Woman, will be held in the Wesleyan Chapel, at Seneca Falls, N. Y., on Wednesday and Thursday the 19th and 20th of July current, commencing at 10 o'clock A. M.

During the first day, the meeting will be exclusively for Women, which all are earnestly invited to attend. The public generally are invited to be present on the second day, when LUCRETIA MOTT, of Philadelphia, and others both ladies and gentlemen, will address the Convention.

The announcement for the Seneca Falls Convention was reproduced afterward in the August 4, 1848, issue of the Seneca County Courier. Three days before the convention, Lucretia Mott warned Stanton that, because of harvest time, "the convention will not be so large as it otherwise might be." Mott was happily proved wrong when 300 people showed up on the first day.

Condition of Women," which she published in 1838. "Men and women were CREATED EQUAL," she exclaimed. "They are both moral and accountable beings, and whatever is *right* for man to do, is *right* for woman."

Stanton and the other four convention organizers were familiar with these and other visionary ideas about women's equality, and they incorporated them into the drafts that were piling up on the tea table. But their decision to organize a convention and to codify their dissatisfaction with women's second-class status in America was both audacious and courageous—an act no less revolutionary than that of America's revolt against Great Britain almost a century before.

Stanton returned home and continued to work on the declaration. She divided the document into two sections: a Declaration of Sentiments, which specified the many forms of inequality that kept women from enjoying the rights of American citizenship, and a set of Resolutions, or measures, to correct that inequality. Shrewdly, she adapted the Declaration of Independence to link women's cause to that powerful symbol of America's struggle for freedom from tyranny. She drafted a preamble, just as the authors of that earlier declaration had done, to list women's grievances.

Like the Founding Fathers, women sought to overthrow an unjust power—the social and political rule of men—that had deprived them of their equal rights and their pursuit of liberty and happiness. She also drew on the natural-rights ideas of the 18th-century British philosopher John Locke. Locke declared that all people, though he did not specify women, were individuals endowed with certain inalienable and natural rights—rights granted not by a king or other ruler who could take them away but by virtue of being human beings. Similarly, insisted Stanton, women are citizens and are entitled to all of the rights and privileges of citizenship.

Then, in a lengthy series of resolutions, she demanded an end to all social, political, and economic discrimination against women. For married women she demanded the right to keep their own property and wages if they worked, and an end to the legal tradition that prevented wives from signing contracts, gave fathers instead of mothers guardianship over their children in divorce proceedings, denied all women a voice in making laws, and compelled wives to obey their husbands in all matters. She also called for greater educational and employment opportunities for women, and insisted that men stop choosing the social roles appropriate to women—a right that "belongs to her conscience and to her God."

Finally she demanded for American women the right to vote. This last demand was the most radical of all, because it directly challenged women's social and political subservience to men and endowed women with the same political power as men. Never before had American women publicly demanded such a right. But for Stanton the right to vote was the right from which all other rights and reforms would follow. The ballot would give women that political power to change laws that were unfair to them. Even Mott, who was committed to women's equality, gasped in shock when Stanton proposed women's right to vote. "Oh, Lizzie," she declared in a letter to Stanton, "thou will make us ridiculous! We must go slowly." But Stanton would not budge, and the demand for women's right to vote stayed in the declaration.

On Sunday, July 16, 1848, the women met again and debated Stanton's declaration. After much deliberation they came up with a final draft, which minced no words: "The history of mankind is the history of repeated injuries and usurpations on the part of man toward woman." The declaration enumerated 16 transgressions against women resulting from men's "absolute tyranny." Like a drum roll, the declaration repeated in powerful, eloquent language the many ways that American women felt "aggrieved, oppressed, and fraudulently deprived of their most sacred rights":

Men had never permitted women to exercise their inalienable right to vote.

They had compelled women to submit to laws, which they had no voice in making.

Men had withheld from women rights that were customarily given to the most "ignorant and degraded" men, meaning free blacks and immigrants.

Having deprived women of the cardinal right of citizenship—the right to vote—men had also deprived women of representation "in the halls of legislation," thereby oppressing them "on all sides."

On the morning of July 19, people streamed into Seneca Falls from all directions. Usually placid, the village buzzed with activity. About 300 people, including 40 men, had converged on the small town. Among them was Charlotte Woodward, a young glove maker who wanted to change the laws that gave husbands the right to pocket their wives' earnings and take over any property they owned. "Most women," she wrote later, "accepted this condition of society as normal and God-ordained and therefore changeless. But... every fibre of my being rebelled.... I wanted to choose my task and I wanted to collect my wages."

Most of the convention's participants lived in Seneca Falls and nearby Waterloo, but others had traveled from Rochester, Auburn, and other surrounding towns. They came out of curiosity and also out of a desire to improve women's lives. Quakers and local Free Soilers—supporters of a new political party opposed to the spread of slavery into territories recently captured from Mexico—attended in

great numbers. But one person who was conspicuously absent was Henry Stanton. Although he had helped to draft some of the resolutions, he was opposed to the woman suffrage resolution, and left town to avoid any political embarrassment from being associated with such folly.

At the Wesleyan Chapel, where the convention was to meet, the organizers decided not to bar men from attending the first day as originally planned—in part because they needed the assistance of a man. None of the five organizers could bring herself to preside over the meeting; they did not believe that was a proper role for women in mixed company. Instead, they asked James Mott, Lucretia Mott's husband, to chair the proceedings. After Mott called the meeting to order, Stanton briefly stated the purpose of the convention. Amelia Bloomer, one of the participants who would soon start publishing a journal, the *Lily*, devoted to temperance and to women's rights, recalled in her journal that Stanton's voice "was weak and timid, and did not reach the remote parts of the house." Stanton was not accustomed to speaking in public, and perhaps the significance of the occasion overwhelmed her.

A view of Seneca Falls around 1848. After the Seneca Falls Convention, Stanton found the village to be more lively and interesting. She started a conversation club to discuss new ideas; open to both men and women, it "brought together the best minds in the community," she said.

During that day and the next, the assembly debated the Declaration of Sentiments and Resolutions. The declaration was adopted by a unanimous vote, but the resolutions, especially the woman suffrage clause, were hotly debated. Frederick Douglass, an ardent supporter of women's rights, stood up and vigorously defended Stanton's demand for the ballot. Douglass supported women's rights as part of a larger quest to achieve freedom and equality for all people, and he regarded women's right to vote as an essential tool for securing female equality. After further debate, the resolution passed by a small margin, and at the end of the final session, 100 women and men—including Charlotte Woodward, the young glove maker—signed the Declaration of Sentiments and Resolutions.

Newspapers across the country carried reports of the Seneca Falls Convention. Much of the coverage was critical, even nasty. One editorial called the convention "the most shocking and unnatural incident ever recorded in the history of womanity." Editors accused female participants of "unwomanly behavior" and of neglecting "their more appropriate duties." They feared that equal rights would "demoralize and degrade" women and "prove a monstrous injury to all mankind."

In spite of these stern denunciations, the Seneca Falls Convention galvanized women to work for their rights. Seneca Falls was the opening salvo of the organized women's rights movement in the United States. Women finally set forth the problem of sexual inequality in all its forms—political, social, economic, and personal. The Declaration of Sentiments and Resolutions became a road map for the path women hoped to travel toward equality and self-determination. It would set the tone and goals of the American women's rights movement for decades to come. More important, the convention brought women together as a group to solve their problems. After Seneca Falls, women would call other conventions and establish local and national organizations to press their claims for equality. From this point on, American women would crusade for their rights behind the banner of an organized movement.

For Stanton, the convention held a more personal significance. For the first time in months, she felt a sense of purpose. To rebut opponents in local and national newspapers, she embarked on a vigorous study of civil and religious law, the Bible, scientific theories, history, and philosophy. "Now my mind, as well as my hands, was fully occupied," she later remarked in her autobiography, "and instead of mourning, as I had done, over what I had lost in leaving Boston, I tried in every way to make the most of life in Seneca Falls."

Stanton wasted no time responding to critics of women's rights. Only four days after the convention, Stanton and Elizabeth McClintock wrote to the *Seneca County Courier* to refute a minister's claim that the Bible commanded women's subservience. "The Bible," they asserted, "is the great charter of human rights, when it is taken in its true spiritual meaning. . . . No reform has ever been started but the Bible, falsely interpreted, has opposed it. . . . Let the people no longer trust to their blind guides, but read and reason for themselves."

Two weeks after the Seneca Falls Convention, Stanton participated in a second women's rights convention in Rochester, New York. Several weeks later, she spoke at a meeting in Waterloo, New York. "Woman herself must do this work," she told her audience. Again, she called for woman suffrage: "The right is ours, have it we must—use it we will." She also exhorted her listeners to recognize women's right and destiny to live as full human beings. "Let woman live as she should, let her feel her accountability to her Maker— Let her know that her spirit is fitted for as high a sphere as man's and that her soul requires food as pure [and] refreshing as his." With every speech she gave and every meeting she attended, Stanton's zest for her work and her commitment to the cause of women's rights deepened.

text continues on page 54

THE DECLARATION OF SENTIMENTS

The Declaration of Sentiments, which was drafted primarily by Stanton and which was adopted at the Seneca Falls Convention, became the blueprint of the 19th-century American women's rights movement. Stanton shrewdly adapted the preamble of the Declaration of Independence to link women's demand for political, social, and economic equality with that powerful symbol of America's struggle for freedom.

When, in the course of human events, it becomes necessary for one portion of the family of man to assume among the people of the earth a position different from that which they have hitherto occupied, but one to which the laws of nature and of nature's God entitle them, a decent respect to the opinions of mankind requires that they should declare the causes that impel them to such a course.

We hold these truths to be self-evident: that all men and women are created equal; that they are endowed by their Creator with certain inalienable rights; that among these are life, liberty, and the pursuit of happiness; that to secure these rights governments are instituted, deriving their just powers from the consent of the governed. Whenever any form of Government becomes destructive of these ends, it is the right of those who suffer from it to refuse allegiance to it, and to insist upon the institution of a new government, laying its foundation on such principles, and organizing its powers in such form as to them shall seem most likely to effect their safety and happiness.... Prudence, indeed, will dictate that governments long established should not be changed for light and transient causes.... But when a long train of abuses and usurpations, pursuing invariably the same object, evinces a design to reduce them under absolute despotism, it is their duty to throw off such government, and to provide new guards for their future security. Such has been the patient sufferance of the women under this government, and such is now the necessity which constrains them to demand the equal station to which they are entitled.

The history of mankind is a history of repeated injuries and usurpations on the part of man toward woman, having in direct object the establishment of an absolute tyranny over her. To prove this, let facts be submitted to a candid world.

REPORT

OF THE

WOMAN'S RIGHTS

CONVENTION,

Held at SENECA FALLS, N. Y., July 19th and 20th, 1848.

ROCHESTER:
PRINTED BY JOHN DICK,
AT THE NORTH STAR OFFICE.
—
1848.

This report of the proceedings at Seneca Falls Convention was printed in the office of the North Star, *the abolitionist newspaper edited by Frederick Douglass, who was also a fervent advocate of women's rights.*

Other women quickly took up the cause and organized their own groups. Like ripples caused by a stone thrown into a pond, activists met one another through other reform efforts or through family and friends. Just as Stanton had met Mott at the World's Anti-Slavery Convention, newcomers to the cause inspired each other to work for women's rights while they were promoting abolition or temperance. Two young activists—Antoinette Brown and Lucy Stone—first met each other in 1846 when they were both students at Oberlin College in Ohio, the first four-year college in the United States to admit women. After Stone graduated in 1847, she joined the American Anti-Slavery Society as a paid lecturer. But almost immediately she began advocating women's rights as well. When leaders of the society objected, she calmly replied, "I was a woman before I was an abolitionist. I must speak for the women." Stone in turn inspired her friend Antoinette Brown to work for woman suffrage.

While other pioneers organized meetings and lectured publicly, Stanton continued to write letters and articles for newspapers and reform journals. Her pen was her most potent weapon. Unable to attend an Ohio women's rights convention on April 7, 1850, because of responsibilities at home, Stanton sent a letter urging the delegates to petition for the right to vote. Stanton also urged the delegates to demand their own representatives in Congress. "Men cannot represent us. They are so thoroughly educated into the belief that woman's nature is altogether different from their own, that they have no idea that she can be governed by the same laws of mind as themselves." Stanton then zeroed in on the legal invisibility of married women and compared them to slaves. "A married woman has no legal existence; she has no more absolute rights than a slave on a Southern plantation. She takes the name of her master, holds nothing, owns nothing, can bring no action in her own name." These were fearless words, and they came from all that Stanton had observed and reflected upon over many years.

The Stantons celebrated their 10th wedding anniversary in May 1850. Both partners felt contented with their lives. They had three healthy, thriving sons, and both of them stood on the cusp of new political careers: Henry Stanton, who had switched political allegiances yet again, was now a Democratic state senator, and Elizabeth Cady Stanton was fast emerging as the leading thinker and strategist of the women's rights movement, though she attended none of the state meetings.

On Sunday evening, February 9, 1851, Stanton gave birth to a robust fourth son, Theodore Weld Stanton. The delivery was easy, and she was back at her desk the next day. "Laugh in your turn," she chortled in a letter to her cousin Elizabeth Smith Miller. "I have actually got my fourth son. Yes, Theodore Weld Stanton...bounded upon the stage of life, with great ease comparatively!! I was sick but a few hours, did not lie down half an hour before he was born.... This morning I got up bathed myself in cold water & have sat by the table writing several letters."

Stanton was a permissive mother. She tried to reason or bribe her sons into good behavior, and resorted to spanking only after all other methods had failed. But the boys remained full of mischief, and she happily called them her "young savages." The three older boys—Daniel, Henry, and Gerrit—were constantly getting into trouble. They leaped off rooftops and slid down lightning rods. Daniel once shot an arrow into Gerrit's eye—fortunately causing no permanent damage—and another time locked Henry in the smoke-house. Yet Stanton remained firmly committed to giving her children as much freedom and independence as they could stand without harming themselves or others.

Shortly before Theodore was born, Stanton and her husband had reluctantly sent their two older sons to a board-ing school run by Theodore D. Weld in Raritan, New Jersey. They were dissatisfied with the quality of the schools in Seneca Falls and believed that Weld, an abolitionist with broad and humane reform interests, would instill the right values. Stanton wrote her sons loving, breezy missives full of news from home. "Spring has come in lazily, dear boys," she penned on May 4, 1851, "but our grass is now green and our trees leafing out.... We shall meet, dear boys, while the flowers are blooming and all nature is happy and joyous. Good night. Mother"

Stanton soon discovered an innovation that made her domestic life easier and also appealed to her growing commitment to women's rights: bloomers, an outfit consisting of long pants worn under a knee-length full skirt. Eight months pregnant with Theodore, Stanton eagerly started wearing the costume and was enthralled by the freedom it gave her. "What incredible freedom I enjoyed!" she recalled in her autobiography. "Like a captive set free from his ball and chain, I was always ready for a brisk walk through sleet and snow and rain, to climb a mountain, jump over a fence, work in the garden, and, in fact, for any necessary locomotion."

To Stanton and other women's rights activists, bloomers were an important improvement in women's lives. Besides offering more freedom of movement, bloomers were far more comfortable and less injurious to a woman's body than tight-bodiced dresses with their layers of petticoats and their rigid steel and whalebone corsets, which prevented easy breathing. And by wearing bloomers, a woman publicly demonstrated her commitment to independent thought and action and her rejection of genteel images of frail womanhood. Bloomers were yet another step forward in promoting women's unfettered movement and action.

But Stanton and other women who wore bloomers paid a heavy price in public ridicule for this newfound freedom and comfort. Henry Stanton's political opponents turned bloomers into a campaign issue during his bid for reelection in 1851. She held firm to her resolve even when her son Daniel asked her not to wear bloomers when she visited him at school because the other boys teased him mercilessly

SENECA FALLS, N. Y., JANUARY, 1852.   NO. 1.

OUR FASHION PLATE. | If our readers are curious to know which

about her unusual dress. "Why, my dear child," she wrote back to him on October 14, 1851, "I have no other [dress]. . . . Now why do you wish me to wear what is uncomfortable, inconvenient, and many times dangerous? I'll tell you why. You want me to be like other people. You do not like to have me laughed at. You must learn not to care for what foolish people say."

As Elizabeth Cady Stanton's commitment to the cause of women's rights deepened, she became much less "like other people." And she certainly paid little attention to what "foolish people" thought about her words or actions. From advocating the vote to wearing bloomers, she boldly set out to combat all forms of sexual inequality.

This picture in the Lily *allegedly shows Stanton (left) and Amelia Bloomer (right), the journal's publisher, dressed in bloomers, a garment designed for women's comfort. Stanton endured intense scorn for wearing bloomers in public but declared that she would never give them up, "for now it involves a principle of freedom."*

Grassmere Saturday

Dear friend,

Allow me to introduce to you Mrs Bloomer of Seneca Falls, Editor of the Lily, a paper devoted to Temperance & Literature, with a sensible infusion of women's rights. Mrs Bloomer wishes to get subscribers to her paper. Will you aid her what you can. We women's rights women ought to do all in our power to sustain every effort in the behalf of women, to open for herself a higher & easier road to fortune & fame, than the old beaten ones of the needle, teaching & marrying as a necessity. That women are beginning to edit papers is a promising sign of the times. Do what you can for the Lily I should think we might get some subscribers in Geneva, what do you think? — Whatever you do for the Lily I shall esteem a personal favor as I feel interested in its success & remain

your much obliged
friend E. C. Stanton

Stanton believed that women should help each other in the struggle to achieve equal rights. In this letter to Amy Kirby Post, a fellow activist, she urges Post to promote Amelia Bloomer's newspaper, the Lily, which she describes as temperance paper "with a sensible infusion of women's rights."

5

"I NEVER FELT MORE KEENLY THE DEGRADATION OF MY SEX"

One early spring evening in May 1851, Stanton attended an antislavery lecture by George Thompson, the fiery British orator who was speaking throughout New York State. While walking home after the lecture, Stanton ran into Amelia Bloomer and a guest of hers, Susan B. Anthony, a temperance activist from Rochester, New York. "There she stood," Stanton recalled in her autobiography, "with her good earnest face and genial smile, dressed in gray delaine, hat and all the same color, relieved with pale blue ribbons, the perfection of neatness and sobriety." Bloomer introduced the two women, and Stanton was instantly impressed. "I liked her thoroughly," she reported.

At first Stanton and Anthony corresponded, mostly about Anthony's temperance activities; she was committed to that cause and had not yet fully converted herself to the cause of women's rights. But gradually their friendship blossomed, and Anthony began spending more time in Seneca Falls. In Anthony, Stanton found an eager, energetic recruit, and Anthony was unabashedly impressed by Stanton's intelligence and writing abilities. Drawn together by circumstance and temperament, they soon forged a powerful partnership for women's rights, a friendship and collaboration that would last for 50 years.

Anthony brought to their partnership a keen mind and an enormous capacity for hard work. Born in 1820 in western Massachusetts, she was raised as a Quaker. Her grandmother and two aunts were influential leaders in the Quaker faith, and young Susan Brownell Anthony was accustomed to hearing women speak their minds. Her parents also encouraged their daughters to think for themselves and to acquire an education. Her father, Daniel Anthony, was an ardent abolitionist, and he urged Susan to take up a social cause. After attending a Quaker seminary near Philadelphia, she taught school for several years in New York State. But teaching did not satisfy her need for intellectual or moral fulfillment, and in 1849 she left her teaching post, moved back home to manage the family farm near Rochester, and joined the temperance and abolition movements.

Initially Stanton and Anthony worked to promote women's participation in the temperance movement, because Stanton felt that temperance was an issue of great concern for women. Banning the consumption of alcohol would help to curb men's drunken, abusive behavior toward their wives and children and prevent them from squandering the family's income on drink. Like many male abolitionists, male temperance leaders often opposed giving female members more visibility in temperance activism. Just as female delegates were not permitted to speak at the World's Anti-Slavery Convention in London in 1840, Anthony was prohibited from speaking at a Sons of Temperance Meeting in Albany, New York, in January 1852. When she rose to speak, one of the male leaders reprimanded her: "The sisters were not invited there to speak but to listen and learn."

Anthony had heard enough, and she angrily marched out of the room, followed by other women. She organized a meeting open only to women, invited newspaper reporters, and announced the formation of a new organization: the

Women's New York State Temperance Society. "We are heartily sick and tired of the round of unmeaning encomiums which Gentlemen Temperance lecturers are pleased to lavish upon our sex," she declared in her remarks to the gathering.

When Anthony scheduled a series of meetings, Stanton wrote to her, "I will do all in my power to aid you. Work down this way, then you come and stay with me." With a little practice, she was sure that Anthony could become "an admirable speaker." She advised her protégé, "Dress loose, take a great deal of exercise & be particular about your diet, & sleep enough. [T]he body has great effect upon the mind. In your meetings if attacked be good-natured & cool, for if you are simple & truth loving no sophistry can confound you."

And so it went. While Anthony was passionately venturing out into that world, emerging as an effective reformer in her own right as well as the messenger of Stanton's ideas, Stanton felt shut out of the world of reform by her burgeoning family responsibilities. Stanton despaired that her many domestic obligations did not allow her adequate time to read, think, and write.

Both Stanton and Anthony faced difficulties in their chosen roles, and their close bond was a mutual source of comfort. "I long to see you, Susan," Stanton wrote during one particularly discouraging period in 1853. "If I had you with me about once a week to rouse my self esteem it would be most beneficial." And when Anthony felt discouraged or overwhelmed by all the travel and meetings,

In photographs, such as this one from 1865, Susan B. Anthony appears a grim and dour woman, but in person and in her correspondence, she was witty and expressive. For her, the ballot was the fundamental right: "What we demand is that woman shall have the ballot, for she will never get her other rights until she demands them with the ballot in her hand."

she turned to her friend: "Dear Mrs. Stanton, How I do long to be with you this very minute—to have one look into your very soul & one sound of your...stirring voice."

Anthony began to spend even more time at Seneca Falls, arriving each time with armfuls of statistics, articles, and legislative reports—which Stanton, like a magician, turned into bold and persuasive speeches. In later years, Anthony wrote most of her own speeches, revealing a keen intellect, but for now she did the research and supplied the facts for the speeches that Stanton wrote. She also became a tireless recruiter for new converts. Her impressive research and organizational skills perfectly complemented Stanton's analytical mind and eloquent pen. Together, they made a powerful team. Henry Stanton put it best when he said to his wife, "You stir up Susan, and she stirs the world." Gleefully, Stanton repeated his words in a letter to Anthony.

In April of 1852, Stanton was elected president of the newly formed Women's New York State Temperance Society, and Anthony became secretary. This was Stanton's first leadership position and the first of several organizational duties that Stanton and Anthony shared. Almost immediately Stanton transformed the temperance organization into a forum for women's rights, because she believed that women's lack of power in marriage prevented them from banning alcohol or gaining political and economic rights.

Stanton believed that drunkenness should be made legal grounds for divorce and that public opinion had to renounce the sentimental idea of marriage as a sacred and untouchable compact, because these ideas entrapped women in loveless and abusive marriages, especially when the husband was alcoholic. In a letter to the inaugural meeting of the society, she declared these demoralizing and degrading unions to be no better than "legalized prostitution."

These were fighting words that brought the wrath of temperance activists who accused Stanton of turning the meeting into a women's rights gathering. Even among temperance and women's rights advocates, Stanton found little support for her ideas; most people, including liberal-minded reformers, regarded marriage as a holy union, a permanent bond consecrated by God and the state. But for Stanton, temperance and women's rights were intimately linked. "Waste no more time in petitioning, until we have men with clear heads and sound hearts in our halls of legislation," she instructed the temperance women of New York State in an appeal on July 1, 1852. "Let woman never again be guilty of the folly of asking wine and beer-drinkers to put down the liquor traffic. When we fill our Senate Chambers with men of our own choosing, it will be full time to petition."

On October 20, 1852, Stanton gave birth to her fifth child—a girl whom she named Margaret Livingston after her own mother. Stanton was ecstatic. "Rejoice with me all Womankind, for lo! a champion of thy cause is born," she wrote Lucretia Mott. "I never felt such sacredness in carrying

This engraving shows a group of women beseeching a saloon keeper to halt the sale of alcohol, but temperance women did more than plead. They lobbied for laws to ban the consumption of alcohol and to protect wives' property and wages from alcoholic husbands. During the 1850s, the temperance and women's rights movements were very closely aligned.

Stanton's belief in dress reform extended to her own young daughter Margaret, who is shown here, with her brother Theodore, comfortably garbed in a loose-fitting sundress with no shoes or stockings. Stanton opposed swaddling infants in tight clothing or blankets as was the custom in the 19th century, preferring instead to give them plenty of freedom to move around.

a child as I have this one, feeling all the time...that I was cherishing the embryo of a mighty female martyr." The infant weighed 12 pounds at birth—"the largest and most vigorous baby I have ever had" —but Stanton's labor was quick and easy.

For Stanton, childbirth was a vital concern that greatly affected the quality of women's lives; she believed that women themselves—not physicians or religious leaders or the tyranny of public opinion—should decide how to dress and give birth. Stanton followed her own instincts and common-sense practices to reduce the pain and incapacitation that traditionally accompanied childbirth.

Throughout that fall and winter, Stanton was occupied with nursing Margaret and caring for her rambunctious sons. With Henry away on political business, the household responsibilities fell mainly on her shoulders. But she read and wrote articles and essays whenever she had a spare moment.

In June 1853, at the first anniversary meeting of the Woman's State Temperance Society, Stanton and Anthony clashed with their co-members over strategy. Stanton was voted out of office, and Anthony resigned her position in support of Stanton. Anthony now realized what Stanton had known all along—that women could never achieve much-needed social reforms until they had political power—and she focused her efforts on achieving women's rights.

Almost immediately, Anthony hounded Stanton for a speech for the upcoming women's rights convention in New York City. But Stanton put her foot down. "Say not one word to me about another convention," she wrote Anthony on June 20, 1853. "I forbid you to ask me to send one thought or one line to any convention, any paper, or any individual; for I swear by all the saints that whilst I am nursing this baby I will not be tormented with suffering humanity." She was determined to put her own house in order first—to hire additional household help, to find a suitable teacher for the boys, and to take good care of Margaret.

Supporters of women's rights had begun to take up their cause with passion and fervor across the North. The New York State Woman's Rights Convention, held in New York City on September 6 and 7, 1853, came to be known as the "mob convention" because male members of the audience at both evening sessions hissed and yelled at speakers on the platform. Cries of "shut up," "take a drink," and "go to bed" filled the huge Broadway Tabernacle. Even Lucretia Mott, who presided over the meeting and was accustomed to unruly mobs from her abolitionist activities, was stunned by the rowdiness. "Never, at any meeting, was public propriety more outraged, than at ours last night," she wrote to a friend. She noted, however, that "not a scream was heard from any woman."

But along with the cranks and critics, the movement drew bold new ideas and speakers. Among the most interesting and unusual allies of women's rights were mediums, spiritualists, and other women who claimed to communicate with the spirit world. The spiritualist movement had begun in the same year, 1848, and in the same region, upstate New York, in which the Seneca Falls Convention was held. Most spiritualists advocated women's right to vote, and many envisioned marriages in which women were equal partners, controlled how many children they wanted, and were free to earn their own wages.

Another activist, Paulina Wright Davis, urged women to be more knowledgeable about their anatomy and reproduction. To combat the ignorance surrounding women's physiology and sexuality, Davis gave public lectures, using a plaster figure of a female nude. Some of her more delicate listeners, however, were shocked by such a display, and either covered their eyes, fled from the room, or fainted. In 1853, Davis also founded one of the first journals devoted to women's rights, the *Una*. "We ask to be regarded, respected, and treated as human beings, of full age and natural abilities," she wrote in the *Una*, "as equal fellow sinners, and not as infants or beautiful angels, to whom the rules of civil and social justice do not apply."

Meanwhile, in the fall of 1854, Susan B. Anthony badgered Stanton to write a speech in favor of expanding New York's Married Woman's Property Act. "I find there is no use saying 'no' to you," Stanton wearily wrote in reply. Juggling her maternal duties with her activist instincts, she finished the speech a few weeks later and delivered it on Valentine's Day, February 14, 1854, at the New York State Woman's Rights Convention. "We demand the full recognition of all our rights as citizens of the Empire State," Stanton said, getting directly to her point. "We are persons; native, free-born citizens; property-holders, tax-payers; yet are we denied the exercise of our right to the elective franchise. We support ourselves, and, in part, your schools, colleges, churches, your poor-houses, jails, prisons, the army, the navy, the whole machinery of government, and yet we have no voice in your councils.... The wife who inherits no property holds about the same legal position that does the slave on the southern plantation. She can own nothing, sell nothing. She has no right even to the wages she earns; her person, her time, her services are the property of another." The delegates were enthralled and adopted the speech as the convention's official address to the legislature. It would be Stanton's last public address for six years.

While Anthony, Mott, Davis, Stone, and others clamored for Stanton to increase her visibility and activity, her father continued to oppose her women's rights work. Even her

ADDRESS

TO THE

Legislature of New-York,

ADOPTED BY THE

STATE WOMAN'S RIGHTS CONVENTION,

HELD AT ALBANY,

Tuesday and Wednesday, February 14 and 15, 1854.

• ● •

PREPARED BY

ELIZABETH CADY STANTON,

Of Seneca Falls, N. Y.

• ● •

ALBANY:
WEED, PARSONS AND COMPANY.
1854.

In her address to the 1854 New York State Woman's Rights Convention, which the delegates adopted as the convention's official address to the state legislature, Stanton compared the legal existence of married women to slaves, who had no rights.

husband, who supported her goals and praised her achievements, pressured her to remain at home, though he continued to travel freely on business. More and more, Stanton bristled at her family's opposition. On September 10, 1855, she wrote Anthony, "I passed through a terrible scourging when last at my father's. I cannot tell you how deep the

The Una *was one of
the first journals devoted
to women's rights. The
editor, Paulina Wright
Davis, a passionate
advocate of women's
equality, declared the
journal's mission was to
"discuss the rights,
sphere, duty and destiny
of woman, fully and
fearlessly."*

iron entered my soul. I never felt more keenly the degradation of my sex. To think that all in me of which my father
would have felt a proper pride had I been a man, is deeply
mortifying to him because I am a woman. That thought has
stung me to a fierce decision—to speak as soon as I can do
myself credit. But the pressure on me just now is too great.
Henry sides with my friends, who oppose me in all that is
dearest to my heart.... But I will both write and
speak.... Sometimes, Susan, I struggle in deep waters."

On January 20, 1856, Stanton gave birth to another
baby girl, Harriot Eaton Stanton. It was a difficult delivery.
Though she was pleased to have another daughter, she also
despaired over the time and energy that she would have to
devote to her family and not to her work. "I feel disappointed
and sad... at this grievous interruption of my plans," she
wrote to Anthony. "I might have been born an orator
before spring, you acting as midwife.... My whole thought
for the present must center on bread and babies."

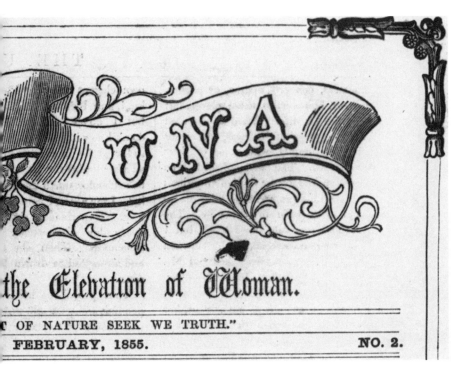

UNA

the Elebation of Woman.

OF NATURE SEEK WE TRUTH."

FEBRUARY, 1855.   NO. 2.

Anthony, however, continued to "midwife" Stanton back into the movement. In June 1856, she pleaded with Stanton to write an address to the New York State Teachers' Convention. Anthony had intended to write the address herself, but she simply felt inadequate for the task.

In the same letter she scolded Stanton and Lucy Stone and Antoinette Blackwell for squandering their talents by giving themselves over to "baby making" and leaving "poor brainless me to battle alone." Anthony was referring to the fever of domesticity that had erupted among women's rights activists. In May 1855, Lucy Stone had married Henry Blackwell, an abolitionist and ardent supporter of women's rights. Although Stone decided to keep her own name and continued to travel and lecture, it was only a matter of time before she would be pregnant. In January 1856, Stone's friend and fellow activist, Antoinette Brown, married Henry Blackwell's brother, Samuel. Antoinette Brown Blackwell even encouraged Anthony to "get a good husband."

In response to Anthony's plea, Stanton calmly wrote, "Come here and I will do what I can to help you with your address, if you will hold the baby and make the puddings." Then she added in defense of Stone and Blackwell's temporary retreat from activism: "You, too, must rest, Susan; let the world alone awhile. We can not bring about a moral revolution in a day or a year. Now that I have two daughters, I feel fresh strength to work for women. It is not in vain that in myself I feel all the wearisome care to which woman even in her best estate is subject."

In spite of Anthony's best efforts to keep stirring things up, by 1857 the movement for women's rights had lurched to a standstill. The question of slavery, always lurking below the surface of public events, had become the nation's most pressing problem. Like a "fire bell in the night," as Thomas Jefferson had written almost four decades earlier, slavery threatened to destroy the nation itself. In Kansas Territory in 1856, a small-scale civil war had erupted between pro- and antislavery groups. By 1857, the debate over the future of slavery had reached a fever pitch because of the U.S. Supreme Court's decision about the status of Dred Scott, a slave. Scott's owner had taken him from a plantation in Missouri, a slave state, to Illinois, a free state, and later to Wisconsin Territory, where slavery was also prohibited. Scott claimed that he was now a free man after residing on free soil. But the Court disagreed and ruled that Congress had no power to exclude slavery from any part of the United States, including its territorial possessions.

Beyond its immediate impact on the unfortunate Dred Scott, the Court's ruling helped to shatter all peaceful attempts to resolve the poisonous question of slavery; instead, it fanned the flames of bitterness between North and South. Stanton herself was convinced that civil war was inevitable. "Our fair republic must be the victim of the monster, slavery, unless we speedily rise in our might and boldly shout freedom," she wrote to her cousin Elizabeth Smith Miller.

Roused from their marital bliss, Lucy Stone, Antoinette Brown Blackwell, and other abolitionists who had also supported women's rights now poured their energies into antislavery agitation. For them, the importance of women's equality paled in comparison to the crisis of slavery. Valiantly, Stanton and Anthony continued to rally awareness for women's rights.

On March 13, 1859, Stanton gave birth to her seventh child, a son. His name was Robert Livingston Stanton, and he weighed a whopping 12 1/4 pounds. Now 43, Stanton was exhausted. Robert was her last child, but his delivery was the most difficult of all. Three weeks after he was born, she wrote Anthony, "My labour was long and very very severe. I never suffered so much before. I was sick all the time before he was born, and I have been very weak ever since. He seemed to take up every particle of my vitality soul and body."

In the fall of 1859, Judge Cady died. His health had been delicate, and he had lost both his hearing and sight. Stanton was bereft. Though she and her father had battled over women's rights, he had been a towering force in her life. His dedication to the law had helped to inspire her own political awakening, even though she ultimately came to very different conclusions about the legal and political status of women. And his love of books and ideas had sparked her own. Although Judge Cady might have wished his daughter to pursue a different vocation, he helped to shape the brilliant thinker and uncompromising fighter that Elizabeth Cady Stanton had become, and she felt his loss keenly.

Shortly after her father's death, Stanton was dealt another blow. On October 16, 1859, John Brown, a fierce opponent of slavery, led a band of 21 men to raid the federal arsenal at Harper's Ferry, Virginia. He intended to distribute the weapons from the arsenal to slaves, who would then rise up to revolt against their masters. Brown, a man of burning

text continues on page 74

"I HAVE ALL THE RIGHTS I WANT"

This pamphlet was published by Stanton anonymously and with no date, but it was available for sale by October 1859. She wanted to combat women's opposition or indifference to the women's rights movement, which disheartened her more than men's resistance. Here she addresses complacent and ignorant women, whom she perceives to be blinded to the oppressive constraints of their lives. She urges women not only to demand their political and economic rights but to throw off the "tyranny of custom"— as expressed in the saying "I have all the rights I want"—and seek lives of purpose and fulfillment, however unconventional their paths might be.

We have allowed this saying from the mouth of woman to pass quite long enough unrebuked, seeing that it is utterly and entirely false, and every woman who utters it knows in her own soul that it is so. . . .

Go watch the daily life of fortune's most favored woman. She has father, husband, brothers, sons, all willing and happy to minister to every wish and want. Luxurious and elegant are her surroundings, peace and plenty seem to mark out every path; but she is not happy—her life is objectless—there is no scope or freedom for the acting out of her womanhood....If she should follow the holy instincts of her nature, she would leave undone many things that mere conventionalism now says she should do, and do many things she ought not to do.

If a woman make a blunder in her marriage, where shall she find happiness? In her children? Maternity has its penalties, many and severe. Bearing children without love is not the highest happiness of which a woman even is capable. What woman, who for peace' sake, has become the mother of five, ten or fourteen children, heirs ofttimes to poverty, disease and suffering, can say with truth, "I have all the rights I want!"...

Go ask the poor widow, childless and alone, driven out from the beautiful home which she had helped to build and decorate, why strangers dwell at her hearthstone, enjoy the shade of trees planted by her hand, drink in the fragrance of her flowers, whilst she must seek some bare and humbler home? Will she tell you she has "all the rights she wants," as she points you to our statute laws, which allow the childless widow to retain a life interest merely in "one-third the landed estate, and one-half the personal property of her husband?"Go ask the wife and mother, who, weary of the heavy yoke of a discordant marriage, in obedience to the holy instincts of true womanhood, sunders the tie that binds her to one she does not love—behold her stripped of children, property and home, for law, in case of separation, gives all these to the husband, will *she* tell you in her days of poverty, desolation and lone-liness, "I have all the rights I want?"

Go to any and every class of women who have had their own bread to earn—the Teacher, the Seamstress, the Drunkard's wife, the Outcast, any who have found out by personal experience the injustice of our laws, and the tyranny of our customs, and none will repel your sympathy, or underrate the importance of our demands, with the silly motto, "I have all the rights I want."

But suppose there are some women who actually have all the rights *they* want, surely that is no reason why they should not feel and plead for those who have them not. Because their soft white hands have never labored, is that a reason why they should not demand a right to wages for those who spend their days in honest toil? When famine has reduced any of the human family almost to starvation, shall I refuse them food because I am not hungry? If I have all I want for body and soul, is it not the best reason in the world why I should generously aid all those who are oppressed, suffering, destitute, friendless and alone? Lives there a woman whose nature is so hard, narrow and selfish, that she can pity no sorrows but those which she has felt in her own person? Or can there be one woman in this nation so ignorant that she really thinks she is already living in the full possession of all the rights that belong to a citizen of a Republic?

religious conviction who believed that his mission was ordained by God, was captured after two days of fighting, tried, and sentenced to hang for treason. Among the abolitionists who had financed Brown's raid was Gerrit Smith. After Brown was captured, Smith became overwrought with guilt and anxiety over his role in the raid. He went temporarily insane and was committed to an asylum. Stanton was heartsick. Smith was not only her beloved cousin but also her mentor. More than any man in her life, more than her husband or her father or her brother-in-law Edward Bayard, he had aroused her passion for reform, and now he was reduced to a state "worse than death," as she wrote Anthony.

When Brown was put to death in early December 1859, Stanton mourned his "glorious martyrdom." She had admired his audacity and courage, and she despaired over the future of abolition. She urged Anthony to come visit her. "It would do me great good to see some reformers just now." She lamented her "dwarfed and perverted womanhood," and told Anthony, "When I pass the gate of the celestials and good Peter asks me where I wish to sit, I will say: 'Anywhere so that I am neither a negro nor a woman. Confer on me, great angel, the glory of white manhood, so that henceforth I may feel unlimited freedom.'"

In spite of the increasing feeling of doom over the issue of slavery, Stanton continued to press for women's rights and the abolition of slavery. On March 19, 1860, in an address to the New York State legislature, she once again compared women's legal status to that of the slave and demanded the right to vote. Although the legislature did not pass a suffrage bill, four days before Stanton spoke, the legislators had already passed an expanded property rights bill. The Married Woman's Property Act of 1860 granted women economic rights not included in the property rights act of 1848. Besides gaining control of "her sole and separate property" in wages or whatever other forms of commerce she engaged in, a married woman could now sign contracts, conduct business, and sue or be sued without her husband's approval. The bill also provided that, in cases of divorce or separation, the mother could be made "joint guardian of her children...with equal powers, rights and duties in regard to them, with the husband," and it granted equal and enlarged property rights to both widows and widowers. This was a major advance in expanding women's property rights, but women still did not have the ballot or a voice in public affairs.

On May 8, 1860, in a speech to the American Anti-Slavery Society on the 30th anniversary of its founding, Stanton linked the cause of women to the cause of freedom for the slave, because, in her words, the mission of the society was not only to free the African slave but to rescue the slaves "of custom, creed and sex"—meaning women. Stanton astutely understood that in American society only white men enjoyed the freedom and privileges that should be the birthright of all Americans, and that they feared extending these same privileges to women and blacks. "For while the man is born to do whatever he can, for the woman and the negro there is no such privilege....The badge of degradation is the skin and sex."

Three days later, at the 10th annual National Woman's Rights Convention, also meeting in New York, Stanton proposed ten resolutions in favor of divorce on the grounds of drunkenness, brutality, or incompatibility between partners. "An unfortunate or ill-assorted marriage," she proclaimed, "is ever a calamity." For women especially, argued Stanton, cruel or loveless marriages are no better than imprisonment because marriage and motherhood are women's only lot in life. "A man, in the full tide of business or pleasure, can marry and not change his life one iota; he can be husband, father, and every thing beside: but in marriage, woman gives up all. Home is her sphere, her realm."

Stanton's speech aroused a torrent of criticism. An editorial in the *New York Tribune* called Stanton's ideas "simply shocking" and wondered how "a modest woman should say" what Stanton had said. The *Evening Post* warned readers that they "will be disgusted with this new dogma" that views marriage as a contract. And the weekly *New York Observer* called the meeting "infidel and licentious" and claimed that resolutions "which no true woman could listen to without turning scarlet, were unblushingly read and advocated by a person in woman's attire, named in the programme as Mrs. Elizabeth Cady Stanton." The reformers, the *Observer* warned, "would turn the world into one vast brothel."

Stanton was startled and unnerved by the intensity of the criticism. But she fiercely defended her ideas and expressed no regret for her provocative words. On June 14, she wrote Anthony, "Come what will, my whole soul rejoices in the truth that I have uttered.... How this marriage question grows on me. It lies at the very foundation of all progress.... My own life, observation, thought, feeling, reason, brought me to the conclusion."

Stanton soon turned her attention to a more explosive matter: the prospect of civil war. On May 18, 1860, a week after Stanton addressed the Woman's Rights Convention, the Republican party helped push the nation closer to war by nominating as its Presidential candidate a little-known lawyer from Illinois named Abraham Lincoln. Lincoln opposed slavery, and especially its expansion beyond the South, but he was no abolitionist. He hoped the system would die from within and had even favored colonization, a movement to return freed slaves to Africa. But Southerners despised him, and as the campaign intensified, they managed to convince themselves that a Lincoln Presidency would destroy their way of life.

Although Henry Stanton had earlier supported another Republican candidate, he switched his allegiance to Lincoln when he won the party's nomination. Both Stantons were jubilant when Lincoln won—not because they personally favored him but because they wanted the South to secede.

Shortly before Thanksgiving, Stanton wrote her sons at boarding school, "I suppose it is the last time we shall be compelled to insult the Good Father by thanking him that we are a slave holding Republic; I hope and look for dissolution."

Lincoln had not even taken office before four states—South Carolina, Mississippi, Florida, and Alabama—seceded. In his carefully crafted inaugural address, Lincoln eloquently pleaded with the rebellious southern states to reconsider. "We are not enemies, but friends. We must not be enemies. Though passion may have strained, it must not break our bonds of affection. The mystic chords of memory, stretching from every battle-field, and patriot grave, to every living heart and hearthstone, all over this broad land, will yet swell the chorus of the Union."

But it was no use. On April 12, 1861, Confederate gunboats attacked Fort Sumter, a U.S. garrison in Charleston harbor. For 33 hours, shells bombarded the fort. Finally the commander, Major Robert Anderson, surrendered, and down went the Stars and Stripes. In its place rose the Confederate stars and bars—and war between the North and the South had begun. Virginia promptly joined the Confederacy, followed by North Carolina, Tennessee, and Arkansas.

Stanton rejoiced at the coming of war. According to Anthony, Stanton could not speak or think of anything but the war. "She is very enthusiastic," Anthony wrote to Wendell Phillips a leading abolitionist and women's rights supporter. "[W]hat a glorious revolution we are in—emancipation must come out of it." Stanton, Anthony, and other women's rights leaders canceled the 11th National Woman's Rights Convention, which had been scheduled to meet in New York City. For the next four years, there would be no more conventions—indeed hardly any talk of women's rights—while the women of both the North and South rallied to support the bloodiest, most tragic conflict in the nation's history.

CALL

FOR A MEETING OF THE

LOYAL WOMEN OF THE NATION.

In this crisis of our Country's destiny, it is the duty of every citizen to consider the peculiar blessings of a republican form of goverment and decide what sacrifices of wealth and life are demanded for its defence and preservation.

The policy of the war, our whole future life, depends on a universal, clearly defined idea of the end proposed, and the immense advantages to be secured to ourselves and all mankind, by its accomplishment.

No mere party or sectional cry, no technicalities of Constitution or military law, no mottoes of craft or policy are big enough to touch the great heart of a nation in the midst of revolution. A grand idea, such as freedom or justice, is needful to kindle and sustain the fires of a high enthusiasm.

At this hour, the best word and work of every man and woman are imperatively demanded. To man, by common consent, is assigned the forum, camp and field. What is woman's legitimate work and how she may best accomplish it, is worthy our earnest counsel one with another.

We have heard many complaints of the lack of enthusiasm among Northern Women ; but, when a mother lays her son on the altar of her country, she asks an object equal to the sacrifice. In nursing the sick and wounded, knitting socks, scraping lint, and making jellies, the bravest and best may weary if the thoughts mount not in faith to something beyond and above it all. Work is worship only when a noble purpose fills the soul.

Woman is equally interested and responsible with man in the final settlement of this problem of self-government; therefore let none stand idle spectators now. When every hour is big with destiny, and each delay but complicates our difficulties, it is high time for the daughters of the revolution, in solemn council, to unseal the last will and testament of the Fathers,—lay hold of their birthright of freedom, and keep it a sacred trust for all coming generations.

To this end, we ask the loyal Women of the Nation to meet in New York, on Thursday, the 14th of May next.

Let the Women of every State be largely represented, both by person and by letter.

There will be two sessions — The first at 10 o'clock, A. M., at the Church of the Puritans (Dr Cheever's), Admittance Free—The second at the Cooper Institute—at 7½ o'clock, P. M., Admittance 25 cents. On behalf of the Woman's Central Committee,

ELIZABETH CADY STANTON.

N. B.—Communications relative to and for the meeting should be addressed to SUSAN B. ANTHONY 48 Beekman St., New York.

Eager to show that Northern women were patriotic and dedicated to the cause of war, Stanton issued this call to form a new organization, which became the Women's Loyal National League. Its members launched an extensive petition campaign to abolish slavery, even in states that fought on the Union side.

"A SIMULTANEOUS CHORUS FOR FREEDOM"

War fever swept across the torn nation. As their husbands and sons drilled and marched and prepared for battle in opposing armies, the women of the North and South also swung into action. Throughout the North, women organized soldiers' aid societies to sew uniforms, assemble medical supplies, and knit scarves, socks, mittens, and other items for Union soldiers. Southern women not only knitted socks, sewed uniforms, and rolled bandages, but they also filled cartridges and made sandbags for barricades. Across the nation, the patriotic women of the North and South eagerly anticipated a quick victory for their side.

In August 1861, Henry Stanton accepted a position as deputy collector at the Customs House in New York City. It was a minor post in the Treasury Department, a reward for his work during the Presidential campaign. His wife was delighted. Now she would be in the whirlwind of activity, on behalf of both the war and women's rights.

Her two oldest sons, Neil and Henry, were old enough to enlist. But Neil had no interest in going off to war and instead took a clerkship on his father's staff at the Customs House. Henry, however, was eager to see action. Stanton appealed to Secretary of State William Seward, an old acquaintance and former New York State senator, to recommend Henry for admission to West Point, the prestigious military academy, because, she wrote, "all his proclivities are to the army." Had Stanton been a man, she might very well have enlisted, so fervent was her own war spirit. "This war is music in my ears," she wrote Seward. "It is a simultaneous chorus for freedom; for every nation that has ever fought for liberty on her own soil is now represented in our army."

As the months dragged on and Union forces suffered their first serious defeats at the Battle of Bull Run in Manassas, Virginia, in July 1861, and in several skirmishes afterward, Stanton angrily turned against Lincoln. In her opinion, he was weak and indecisive, and too slow in ending slavery. "All his messages have been of the most mamdy-pamby order," she wrote Gerrit Smith in December 1861 after having read Lincoln's address to Congress. "He certainly does not dignify the office he fills."

In her turn, Susan B. Anthony bristled over the willing-ness of Stanton, Mott, and other activists to suspend all women's rights efforts during the war. Anthony was espe-cially alarmed because many of the victories they had labored so long to achieve were coming unraveled. The New York State legislature had recently amended the 1860 Married Woman's Property Act; although it now allowed women to buy or sell their own property without their hus-bands' consent, it took away a mother's right to equal guardianship of her children if she was legally separated from her husband and eliminated a widow's control over her property—rights that Stanton, Anthony, and their com-rades had struggled to achieve.

Stanton and Anthony managed to patch up their differ-ences over strategy and found a goal they could both agree on—creating a way for Northern women to help end slavery. Women on both sides were already contributing to the war effort in vital ways by working as battlefield nurses, factory hands in the production of war supplies, and government clerks and copyists—jobs that men had occupied before the war. Even Anthony temporarily returned to Massachusetts to take over grueling farm chores so her brothers could join the Union army.

But both Stanton and Anthony believed that Northern women had to play a more direct role in ending slavery. On January 1, 1863, Lincoln issued the Emancipation Proclamation, which freed all slaves in the states that were "in rebellion against the United States"—meaning the Confederate states. The proclamation said nothing about the slaves who toiled in slave-holding states that remained in the Union—Delaware, Maryland, Kentucky, and Missouri—because Lincoln did not want to provoke these states to go over to the Confederate side. Nonetheless, with one stroke of the pen, the President had now turned the Civil War into a war to end slavery as well as to preserve the Union.

Nursing was one of several important occupations that opened up to women during the Civil War. Both Union and Confederate nurses performed valiantly under crude, unsanitary conditions in makeshift field hospitals.

But for Stanton, Anthony, and other abolitionists, this was not enough. Stanton and Anthony decided that the only way to demonstrate Northern women's commitment to abolishing slavery was by creating a national organization. On April 10, 1863, they issued a "call for a meeting of the Loyal Women of the Nation" to create this new organization. The first meeting of the new organization took place on May 14, 1863, at a church in New York City. During this and a subsequent meeting on May 28, delegates voted by a slim majority to

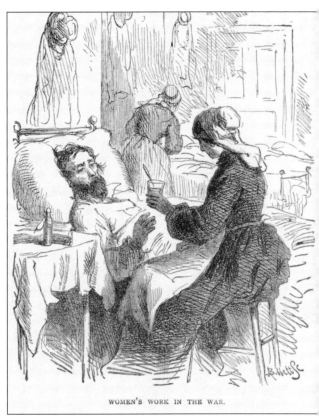

WOMEN'S WORK IN THE WAR.

include women's rights as part of their program. They also named the organization the Women's Loyal National League and pledged themselves to secure 1 million signatures on a petition urging the U.S. Congress to free all slaves in the United States, including those in Union states.

By now Stanton was living in a brownstone at 75 West 45th Street in New York City. On the night of July 13, 1863, the war came right to her front door. Two days before, on Saturday, July 11, draft officers in New York City had begun drawing names from a pool of eligible men. Those chosen were immediately registered in the Union army. This draft, the first in the nation's history, had been authorized by Congress to fill the ranks of the army. The bill also stipulated that men from wealthy families could avoid the draft by paying a fee of $300.

By Sunday evening, July 12, hundreds of angry men, many of them poor Irish immigrant workers, flocked to bars and threatened to attack the draft offices. The next day, they went on a rampage, looting and setting fire to businesses and the offices of Republican newspapers. Rioters beat several black residents, lynched six more, and plundered or destroyed homes or businesses owned by blacks. Less than two blocks from Stanton's home, they burned to the ground the Colored Orphan Asylum. Shouting "Down with the rich" and "there goes a $300 man," they also attacked any well-dressed white men who had the misfortune of being out in public.

While Stanton watched in horror, a group of rioters seized her son Neil, who was standing in front of the house. As they surrounded him, they shouted, "Here's one of those three-hundred-dollar fellows." Panic-stricken, Stanton watched helplessly as they dragged Neil away. Unbeknownst to Stanton, her quick-witted son placated his kidnappers by offering to buy them a round of drinks and joining them in

text continues on page 84

AN APPEAL TO THE WOMEN OF THE REPUBLIC

On April 10, 1863, Stanton and Anthony called for a "meeting of the Loyal Women of the Nation." They wanted to demonstrate Northern women's commitment to abolishing slavery by creating an organization dedicated to that goal. Stanton followed up the call with an article in the April 24 issue of the New York Tribune titled "To the Women of the Republic." She hoped to inspire Northern women to support the war as a crusade to end slavery, and, ever vigilant for any opportunity to promote women's rights, she shrewdly linked the injustice of sexual inequality to this goal.

When our leading journals, orators, and brave men from the battlefield complain that Northern women feel no enthusiasm in the war, the time has come for us to speak—to pledge ourselves loyal to Freedom and our Country....

If it be true that at this hour, the women of the South are more devoted to their cause than we to ours, the fact lies here. They see and feel the horrors of the war; the foe is at their firesides; while we, in peace and plenty, live and move as heretofore. There is an inspiration, too, in a definite purpose, be it good or bad. The women of the South know what their sons are fighting for. The women of the North do not. They appreciate the blessings of Slavery; we do not the blessings of Liberty. We have never yet realized the glory of those institutions in whose defense it is the high privilege of our sires and sons this day, to bleed and die....

Let every woman understand that this war involves the same principles that have convulsed the nations of the earth from Pharaoh to Abraham Lincoln—Liberty or Slavery—Democracy or Aristocracy—Christianity or Barbarism—and choose this day, whether our republican institutions shall be placed on an enduring basis, and an eternal peace secured to our children, or whether we shall leap back through generations of light and experience and meekly bow again to chains and slavery.

three cheers for Jeff Davis, the president of the Confederacy. Fearing the worst, Stanton fled with her younger children and servants to the family home in Johnstown. The riot in New York City lasted a few more days until federal troops from Pennsylvania arrived to restore order.

After the draft riot had subsided, Stanton returned to New York and resumed her work for the Women's Loyal National League. By September 1863, the league had designed a membership badge, showing a black male slave half rising and breaking his own chains, which, Stanton hoped, "every loyal woman in the nation" would wear. By now the tide of war had turned in favor of the Union army. In July 1863, the Union army had stopped a Confederate advance at the Battle of Gettysburg in Pennsylvania. Despite the enormous losses in manpower, Union troops managed to achieve a decisive victory. From this battle, Union forces would begin slowly but steadily to conquer the South and destroy the Southern army.

The Women's Loyal National League lasted for little more than a year, until August 1864, and did not gain significant public support. The *New York Herald* declared that the league had been "originally designed for the most patriotic and praiseworthy motive" but had now degenerated into a "revolutionary women's rights movement." It urged the leaders to "beat a hasty retreat" and stop such "nonsense and tomfoolery." Nonetheless, the league sent its first 100,000 signatures in favor of abolition to Senator Charles Sumner, an ardent abolitionist from Massachusetts, on February 1, 1864. By the time it disbanded, the league had collected 400,000 signatures. Senator Sumner, who presented the league's petitions to the Senate, later credited the league with having spurred on Congress to pass the 13th Amendment, which abolished slavery.

Events moved quickly toward a Union victory. When Lincoln stepped forward on a windy, gloomy March day in 1865 to take the Presidential oath of office once again, victory was in sight. On April 9, 1865, Robert E. Lee, commander of what was left of the Confederate forces, surrendered to General Ulysses S. Grant, commanding officer of the Army of the Potomac. In the North, church bells pealed as crowds filled the streets. But the cost of victory had been huge: the South was physically devastated, and more than 600,000 Union and Confederate soldiers, one in five, had been killed.

Almost 50 and beyond her reproductive years, Stanton plunged into the work for women's rights. She and Anthony confidently believed that women's contributions to the war effort and to ending slavery would soon be repaid with the right to vote. They also believed that their male comrades in the abolition movement, such as Wendell Phillips, Stanton's cousin Gerrit Smith, and Frederick Douglass—all strong women's rights advocates who wielded great influence in shaping postwar Reconstruction policies—would use their powerful political connections to promote women's rights, especially the right to vote. Stanton, Anthony, and their comrades now referred to this right as woman suffrage.

But their hopes were quickly dashed, and Stanton soon realized their cause was in trouble. Newly elected to lead the American Anti-Slavery Society, Wendell Phillips minced no words in telling Stanton that he and other abolitionist allies planned to put woman suffrage on hold while they worked for black male suffrage. He supported women's right to vote, but, he explained in a letter to Stanton, "As Abraham Lincoln said, 'One war at a time'; so I say, One question at a time. This hour belongs to the negro." Enraged, Stanton replied, "May I ask just one question based on the apparent opposition in which you place the negro and the woman? My question is this: Do you believe the African race is composed entirely of males?"

By August 1865, Stanton was alarmed by the dwindling support for woman suffrage and urgently summoned Anthony. "Dear Susan," she wrote, "I have argued constantly with Phillips and the whole fraternity, but I fear one and all will favor enfranchising the negro without us. Woman's cause is in deep water.... [T]here is pressing need of our Woman's Rights Convention. Come back and help. There will be a room for you. I seem to stand alone."

Throughout the summer of 1865, drafts of the 14th Amendment began to circulate. The proposed amendment called for the enfranchisement of black men. Stanton was outraged when she read one such draft. Not only did the amendment focus on the political rights of freedmen while ignoring women's rights, it actively excluded women. "If that word 'male' be inserted [in the 14th Amendment]," she angrily wrote to Gerrit Smith, "it will take us a century at least to get it out again."

Stanton desperately tried to reason with Wendell Phillips that granting black men political and economic rights without granting black women the same rights was akin to "another form of slavery." "If our rulers have the justice to give the black man Suffrage," she wrote to Phillips, "woman should avail herself of that new-born virtue to secure her rights."

Meanwhile, Stanton and Anthony drew up and circulated a petition for woman suffrage. It was the first women's rights petition to be addressed to the United States Congress rather than to individual state legislatures, because Congress was taking up the debate over suffrage and drafting new laws to protect the rights of African Americans. Stanton and Anthony managed to collect 10,000 signatures to submit to Congress by January 1866. But neither the Republicans nor the Democrats in Congress were willing to consider woman suffrage, and they refused to present the petitions to the full Congress.

Casting about for a more effective strategy, Stanton and her allies decided to take the lead in achieving suffrage for both blacks and women rather than wait for Congress to act. As part of their strategy, they urged the American Anti-Slavery Society to merge with the women's rights movement into one national organization.

THE ELEVENTH
National Woman's Rights Convention.

THE Eleventh National Woman's Rights Convention will be held in the City of New York, at the Church of the Puritans, Union Square, on Thursday, the 10th of May, at 10 o'clock.

Addresses will be delivered by persons to be hereafter announced.

Those who tell us the republican idea is a failure, do not see the deep gulf between our broad theory and partial legislation ; do not see that our Government for the last century has been but the repetition of the old experiments of class and caste. Hence, the failure is not in the principle but in the lack of virtue on our part to apply it.

The question now is, have we the wisdom and conscience, from the present upheavings of our political system, to reconstruct a government on the one enduring basis that has never yet been tried—EQUAL RIGHTS TO ALL."

From the proposed class legislation in Congress, it is evident we have not yet learned wisdom from the experience of the past ; for while our representatives at Washington are discussing the right of suffrage for the black man, as the only protection to life, liberty and happiness, they deny that "necessity of citizenship" to woman, by proposing to introduce the word "male" into the Federal Constitution. In securing suffrage but to another shade of manhood, while we disfranchise fifteen million tax-payers, we come not one line nearer the republican idea. Can a ballot in the hand of woman, and dignity on her brow, more unsex her than do a sceptre and a crown ? Shall an American Congress pay less honor to the daughter of a President than a British Parliament to the daughter of a King ? Should not our petitions command as respectful a hearing in a republican Senate, as a speech of Victoria in the House of Lords ? Do we not claim that here all men and women are nobles,—all heirs apparent to the throne ? The fact that this backward legislation has roused so little thought or protest from the women of the country, but proves what some of our ablest thinkers have already declared, that the greatest barrier to a government of equality, is found in the aristocracy of its women. For while woman holds an ideal position above man, and the work of life, poorly imitating the pomp, heraldry and distinctions of an effete European civilization, we as a nation can never realize the divine idea of equality that man in his highest moments has enunciated to the world.

To build a true republic, the church and the home must undergo the same upheaving we now see in the State ;—for while our egotism, selfishness, luxury and ease are baptized in the name of him whose life was sacrifice,—while at the family altar we are taught to worship wealth, power and position, rather than humanity, it is vain to talk of a republican government :—The fair fruits of liberty, equality and fraternity must be blighted in the bud, till cherished in the heart of woman.

At this hour the nation needs the highest thought and inspiration of a true womanhood infused into every vein and artery of its life ;—and woman needs a broader, deeper education, such as a pure religion and lofty patriotism alone can give. From the baptism of this second revolution, should not woman come forth with new strength and dignity, clothed in all those "rights, privileges and immunities" that shall best enable her to fulfil her highest duties to Humanity, her Country, her Family and Herself.

In behalf of the National Woman's Right's Central Committee.

ELIZABETH CADY STANTON, Pres.

SUSAN B. ANTHONY, Sec.

New York (48 Beekman st.,) March 31, 1866.

In this announcement for the first woman's rights convention to be held after the Civil War, Stanton calls on the nation to fulfill the war's lofty goal—the creation of a "true republic" with equal rights for all—by extending the ballot to women as well as to black men. That became the goal of the American Equal Rights Association (AERE), which was organized at this convention.

In May 1866, the 11th National Woman's Rights Convention—the first since the end of the war—came to order in New York City. It was to be a reunion of all the leading prewar figures as well as a platform for new ideas and advocates of women's rights. After Anthony proposed in a speech that the delegates "broaden our Woman's Rights platform, and make it in *name*—what it ever has been in *spirit*—a Human Rights platform," the delegates unanimously voted to change the organization's name to the American Equal Rights Association (AERA).

They elected Lucretia Mott president and Stanton first vice president. Up to now, women had organized conventions and circulated petitions, but the AERA was the first organization committed to achieving women's right to vote. Stanton and Anthony were buoyant about their prospects for success, certain that women would achieve the right to vote when black men did. The AERA's tactics did not move prominent male abolitionists, however. In June 1866, Congress passed the 14th Amendment, which granted black men specifically the right to vote, and sent it on to the states for ratification.

Stanton could see the goal of universal suffrage slipping from her grasp and desperately tried another approach. Claiming that the Constitution did not actually prevent women from holding office even if they could not vote, she declared herself an independent candidate for Congress from New York City's 8th District; boldly, she became the first woman to seek office in the United States Congress. Arguing that neither the Democratic nor the Republican party valued the rights of all citizens, she called for "universal suffrage."

Stanton's motives were not entirely altruistic. Although she skillfully gave lip service to equal rights for all, Stanton believed that the votes of educated women would patriotically protect the nation from the ignorance of African-American or foreign-born male voters. She was appalled that educated women could not vote while the most illiterate man could. "In view of the fact that the Freedmen of the South and the millions of foreigners now crowding our Western shores... are all...to be enfranchised...the best interests of the nation demand that we outweigh this incoming pauperism, ignorance and degradation, with the wealth, education, and refinement of the women of the republic." Stanton received only 24 votes, an overwhelming loss.

Stanton, Anthony, and Lucy Stone now turned their attention to achieving woman suffrage within each state. Stone appeared before a committee of New Jersey legislators to urge lawmakers to remove the words "white male" from the part of the state constitution that specified voting rights. Stanton did the same in New York State, and she and

Anthony sent out similar appeals to the state legislatures of Kansas, Maine, Massachusetts, and Ohio.

Opposed by state representative Horace Greeley, who was also the powerful editor of the *New York Tribune,* Stanton and her allies lost the battle in New York. Stanton managed to alienate Greeley by her tactics. In a letter to her friend Martha Wright, she described her confrontation with Greeley: While she was arguing for women's right to vote, Greeley interrupted her and asked, "The ballot and the bullet go together. If you vote, are you ready to fight?" She replied tartly, "Yes, we are ready to fight, sir, just as you did in the late war, by sending our substitutes." She was pointedly referring to the wealthy men who had avoided military service in the war by hiring a substitute for $300. Stanton further angered Greeley when she and Anthony presented him with a petition for woman suffrage with his wife's signature on it.

The next battleground was Kansas. In March 1867, the Kansas state legislature approved two separate measures for the male voters of Kansas to decide: one to remove the word "white" from the state constitution, and the other to remove the word "male." Just as Kansas had been a testing ground before the Civil War to determine if people supported slavery or freedom within its boundaries, it now became a test to determine public support for woman suffrage.

Although Stanton and Anthony accompanied George Francis Train on a lecture tour of eastern cities, it was an uneasy alliance. An independent candidate for President of the United States, Train used bawdy and racist humor in his flamboyant campaign speeches to pit women's rights against blacks' rights.

The American Equal Rights Association immediately dispatched members to rally the sparsely settled state on behalf of both woman and black male suffrage. In September 1867, Stanton and Anthony took over for the final two months before the election. Splitting up, they covered different regions of the state, but both women endured dreadful hardships. Stanton traveled throughout the state with the governor in a wagon drawn by two mules. She spoke in log cabins, depots, rough-hewn churches and schoolhouses, and outside in the open air, wherever they could gather a handful of voters. One night Stanton spoke in a large mill. The only light came from a candle beside her and a few lanterns scattered about. All she could see of her audience were the whites of their eyes.

Kansas had a strong record in support of women's rights. Only New York State offered women more legal rights. In addition, Kansas women were accustomed to speaking out for themselves and fighting for their beliefs. They were, according to Stanton, "ready for the new doctrine of woman suffrage." As Henry Blackwell wrote to Anthony and Stanton early in the Kansas campaign, "Kansas is to be the battleground for 1867." But the state's Republicans did not share the popular support for women's rights, and the state Republican committee supported only the black suffrage amendment.

As support for woman suffrage unraveled among Kansas Republicans, Stanton and Anthony turned to the state's Democrats. The Democratic State Committee opposed both black and woman suffrage, but there were many Democrats who were willing to support woman suffrage alone. To their allies in the American Equal Rights Association, Stanton and Anthony had committed treason by crossing over to the enemy, the Democrats. After all, the Republicans represented the party of Lincoln—the party that opposed slavery and advocated equal rights for blacks, if only for black men—while the Democrats were the party of the slaveholder.

To make their treason complete, Stanton and Anthony joined forces with George Train, a shrewd railroad developer and racist who fervently believed that whites were superior to blacks. He pitted women's rights against black rights and argued that giving women—specifically white women—the vote would protect whites' social and political power over blacks. Lucy Stone denounced him as a lunatic. Writing to Anthony, William Lloyd Garrison, the venerable abolitionist editor of the *Liberator,* declared himself to be "mortified and astonished beyond measure in seeing Elizabeth Cady Stanton and Susan B. Anthony traveling about the country with that crack-brained harlequin."

Feeling utterly abandoned by their former allies in the Republican party, Stanton and Anthony felt they had no choice but to turn to Train. Privately, Stanton wrote Martha Wright that she was willing to "accept aid even from the devil himself, provided he did not tempt us to lower our standard." In the end, both referendums lost. Only one-third of Kansas's voters supported black suffrage, and woman suffrage received even fewer votes. Slowly, it dawned on Stanton and Anthony that they could no longer rely on their former abolitionist comrades to help them gain the right to vote. Instead, they would have to find new allies and new sources of support. And in that search they would give birth to a new, independent women's rights movement.

The Revolution.

PRINCIPLE, NOT POLICY: JUSTICE, NOT FAVORS.—MEN, THEIR RIGHTS AND NOTHING MORE: WOMEN, THEIR RIGHTS AND NOTHING LES[S]

VOL. I.—NO. 16.　　　NEW YORK, THURSDAY, APRIL 23, 1868.　　　$2 A YEAR.
SINGLE COPY 10 CENT[S]

The Revolution.

ELIZABETH CADY STANTON,　}
PARKER PILLSBURY,　　　　} Editors.
SUSAN B. ANTHONY, Proprietor.

OFFICE 37 PARK ROW (ROOM 17).

THEODORE DREAMING, WITH FLAG AT HALF MAST.

LAST week's *Independent*, in a long column, throws Mr. Chase overboard, clears the track for Grant, and gets itself ready to wheel into line with the multitude in the coming contest. After the most unequivocal praise of "the Chief Justice," the "President of the Senate," "Salmon P. Chase," after making a profound bow to him in each of these capacities, admitting "that his life-long convictions have been in favor of liberty, justice and equality; that he holds to the civil and political rights of all American citizens, without distinction of color or sex," Mr. Tilton winds up by saying his advocacy of Mr. Chase for President now ends, because he has reason to believe that he would accept a nomination from the democratic party.

In the beginning of the new year the *Independent* unfurled its banner to the breeze with universal suffrage for all men and women, of every color and clime, inscribed thereon; and this has been the editor's theme in all his lyceum lectures during the past winter, thus added to his personal admiration for the Chief Justice. Mr. Tilton occupies the same political platform with him, and that makes this sudden divorce the more extraordinary, assuming that the editor of a leading religious journal is governed in all things by moral principle.

There has been a little game going on in certain republican circles hostile to Chase, to prove that he always was a good democrat, and urging the democracy to take him up, thus to get one stumbling-stone out of the way of the Chicago Convention. The leaven, it seems, is beginning to work, and the *Independent* rushes bravely to the ramparts and hauls down the flag for Chase; but this act, by its own showing, is by no means a logical sequence of its estimate of the man. But, unfortunately for all concerned, the wily democrats do not snap at the bait, and the republicans, with their Chief Justice, robes and all, are in as great a quandary as was the immortal Pickwick with the horse he feared to mount. From the stand-[point of principle the question might be ...] stitute another name, it might be the name of Charles Sumner, or Schuyler Colfax, or Ben Wade, or Gen. Butler. But, of course, the Chicago Convention will go poll mell for Gen. Grant. Nevertheless, we shall go on dreaming our day-dream of the happy day when only a great statesman shall be eligible to preside over the Great Republic.

This happy day is to be ushered in by teaching the people how to choose their leaders; that the best interests of the nation do not depend on the success of any party, but on the virtue and education of the people. Why go "pell-mell" for Grant when all admit that he is unfit for the position? It is not too late, if true men and women will do their duty, to make an honest man like Ben Wade President. Let us save the nation. As to the Republican party, the sooner that is scattered to the four winds of Heaven the better. If those who speak every week to 75,000 subscribers "dream" when they should be wide awake and at work, "a Great Republic to preside over" will soon be a dream also.　　　　E. C. S.

ANNA WIDE AWAKE WITH BANNERS FLYING.

THE heroic young orator, Anna E. Dickinson, spent several hours with us last week on her way to Western New York to fill a series of engagements, and promises us a day or two on her return.

The severity of her western work compelled her to rest a few days at home, but we are happy to say she is now herself again, and fulfilling her remaining appointments. We found her as earnest, prophetic and inspirational as ever, having no faith in Grant or the impeachment of the President by the republican party. This intuitive girl sees through all the political shams now going on at Washington. It may be well to delude THE PEOPLE, groaning under the effects of war and taxation, with the idea that this trial is to bring them some relief; but those who see behind the scenes *know* that our present leaders have no appreciation of the nation's danger, or care for the necessities of the laboring classes.

The tyranny of capital and the narrow selfishness of the monied classes reveal a more hideous type of slavery than that of chattelism on the Southern plantation.

THE RADICAL IN A FOG.

THE *Radical*, reviewing Gail Hamilton's "Women's Wrongs, a Counter Irritant," says: Our author has the rare merit of seeing both sides of more easily led *en masse* than the more cultivated Howards.

People who see two right sides to a ques[tion] generally fail to see either side clearly. questions of importance, such as relate to man rights, are so perfectly clear to those who see them at all, that both the right and wrong side stand out in bold relief. It se[ems] to us that neither Gail Hamilton nor her revie[wer] comprehends the deep significance of this q[ues]tion of universal suffrage. In reading [the] book we were struck with its weakness; the [mo]ment the author lost sight of Todd and un[der]took to reason. Like the cat with a mouse, [she] was wide awake and intensely active until [her] victim was no more; then came a reaction [that] left her foggy and dull through many inter[ven]ing pages, until at the close she awoke f[rom] her nap and ascended into the higher real[m of] prophesy and speculation. After boldly ass[ert]ing woman's right to suffrage, we were [sur]prised at the flippant way in which she [dis]posed of woman's duty and dignity in the [exer]cise of their political rights. After annih[ilat]ing the Rev. Todd and clearing the ba[ck]ground of all the trash and rubbish, instead of rebuilding on the spot some ma[jestic] pillar to the new idea, she sits down beside [the] dying Todd and confesses that although [she] has pierced him through and through to m[ain]tain woman's right to suffrage, yet its valu[e in] the regeneration of the race is not worth [the] strength she had spent to prove it. She [is] stung to action by Todd's insults to her [sex.] These she felt, but she did not perceive that w[hat] Todd said was the logical sequence of such a public sentiment as she herself ech[oes] in her foggy presentation of what her revie[wer] calls the other side of the question. [The] strongest way to maintain a right is to sh[ow] the damage done in its denial. Now, if wom[an] would not use the ballot, and be none the be[tter] for its possession, why contend for the rig[ht?] Why contend for the right to embrace a v[ice] when it would be folly or death to exercise [it?]

The admission of woman to the polls [will] essentially change the character of our legi[sla]tion, because then we shall have both the m[ale] and female idea represented in our laws [and] government. Force and selfishness will be [in]corporated with the higher, purer principle[s of] love and sacrifice. "Biddy" will counter[bal]ance with her loving mercy the stern justice [of] "Patrick," and "Mrs. Percy Howard," bei[ng a] strong-minded, conscientious woman, will [love] her country as well as her household, and [will] feel the deepest interest in clearing up [the] great wilderness of life, in plucking the th[orns] from the ten thousand paths where her s[ex]

The Revolution *promoted all aspects of the struggle for female equality, from exposing employment discrimination to advocating women's right to control their own bodies and sexual relations with their husbands. As the paper's senior editor, Stanton wrote many of the articles.*

CHAPTER

7

"WE ARE READY, WE ARE PREPARED"

The first step that Stanton and Anthony took toward creating a new women's rights movement was to establish their own newspaper. Funds for this venture came from George Train. Stanton had tried to start a women's rights journal ever since the end of the war but could not raise enough money. During the Kansas campaign, Train had come up with the name for their journal—the *Revolution*. It expressed Stanton's vision perfectly. She devised the motto on its masthead: "Men, their rights and nothing more. Women, their rights and nothing less."

The first issue appeared on January 8, 1868. The eight-page newspaper resembled a small magazine. Articles and editorials about women's rights mostly filled the first six pages, and the topics covered a variety of issues—divorce reform, the status of women tailors, suffrage activities in Colorado, women's rights in Europe, and prostitution. Parker Pillsbury, the former editor of the *Anti-Slavery Standard,* served as a coeditor and brought valuable editorial expertise. He covered other political events such as the impeachment of President Andrew Johnson and the upcoming political conventions of 1868. George Train and another columnist,

David Melliss, used the last two pages of the *Revolution* to offer their political views and gossipy news of Wall Street scandals.

Stanton and Anthony sold 10,000 copies of the first issue. The reviews were mixed. One reviewer called it "plucky, keen, and wide awake although...not altogether to our taste." Another reviewer found it "sharp and spicey." Soon after the first issue appeared, George Train left for Ireland, and Stanton and Anthony assumed the financial as well as the editorial burdens of running the paper.

As the sun rose over the East River, Stanton and Anthony were usually still at work in the *Revolution*'s spacious first-floor office on East 23rd Street, padding about on the carpeted floor. Engravings of Lucretia Mott and Mary Wollstonecraft, the famed 18th-century English women's rights leader, adorned the white walls, and a bookcase stood at one end filled with books and tracts on women's rights.

The newspaper quickly established itself as a mouthpiece for some of the most prominent and provocative thinkers of the women's rights movement. Matilda Joslyn Gage, Paulina Wright Davis, and Ernestine Rose—all highly dedicated and visionary leaders for women's rights—were regular correspondents. More important, under Stanton's direction the paper dealt with controversial issues—including abortion, regulation of prostitution, divorce, and prison reform—that other periodicals touched upon gingerly, if at all.

Stanton continued to advocate more liberal divorce laws and better legal protection for married women and argued that giving women the vote would rectify the legal and economic inequality of married women. She also championed "self-sovereignty"—her term for women's right to control their own bodies and sexual relations with their husbands. On the *Revolution*'s pages, Stanton boldly set forth an astonishing platform of revolutionary change for women's lives. When there was talk of changing the *Revolution*'s name to something less provocative, Stanton refused. While traveling out West, she wrote to Anthony, "There could not be a better name than *Revolution*. The establishing of woman on her rightful throne is the greatest revolution the world has ever known or ever will know."

As they moved away from the orbit of their former abolitionist allies, Stanton and Anthony looked for new supporters. They soon discovered a potent and hitherto overlooked source of support—working-class women—and took up their cause. Stanton and Anthony were shocked by the hardships these women endured. They learned that factory women worked 10 to 12 hours a day, usually in crowded, unventilated, poorly lit buildings, for wages of less than a dollar a day. Female workers operated dangerous machinery and were allowed no breaks except to snatch a bit of lunch.

Women who did piecework at home and were paid by the item fared no better; in New York City, sewing women were paid four cents for each pair of undershorts they made. Although the sewing machine, which had been invented in 1846, speeded up their work, they still could make only about five pairs a day. For a full day's work, their efforts earned them 20 cents. On top of that, they had to pay for heat, light, and thread, reducing their final pay even more. At this time, the cheapest rooms in New York City cost about a dollar a week. After paying their rent, they had only a few cents left over for food, clothing, medicine, and transportation. As a result, many single women shared rooms and even beds with other workingwomen. Even with this arrangement, they barely had enough money left for food.

The plight of these women workers moved Stanton and Anthony to take action. During 1868, they reported on the unfair treatment of women typesetters who were hired by the owners of the *New York World* to replace striking male typesetters. Once the strike was over, management rehired the men and dismissed the women or found lower-paying jobs for them in other areas of the printing industry. In an editorial in the September 10, 1868, issue, the *Revolution*

Like these women at work in a watch-making factory in Waltham, Massachusetts, women in the post–Civil War period found new employment opportunities in industry—along with dangerous and exploitative working conditions and meager wages.

linked the women's unjust treatment to their lack of voting power. "[T]hey are disfranchised classes, hence degraded in the world of work."

One week later, the *Revolution* became the founding site of the Working Woman's Association (WWA), an organization open to all laboring women. But most of the members were women typesetters and other female laborers in the printing industry. The Working Woman's Association hoped to attain equal wages and better working conditions for women workers. A few weeks later, at Anthony's suggestion, women typesetters in the Working Woman's Association formed a separate group, the Women's Typographical Union. They wanted to establish a women's print shop where all the workers shared in the profits.

Stanton and Anthony offered organizing strategies, meeting space at the *Revolution*'s office, coverage of the meetings in their newspaper, and rousing enthusiasm. In their newspaper's columns, they advocated fair wages, an eight-hour workday, and an end to Wall Street schemes and scandals that enriched a few industrial leaders and financiers at the expense of the working poor. But the commendable goals shared by Stanton and Anthony and the members of the Working Woman's Association could not mask important differences. Stanton and Anthony continued to regard the ballot as the prime tool for achieving the goals of the WWA. In contrast, members such as Emily Peers, a typesetter and leader of the WWA, never considered suffrage to be, in her words, "the great panacea for the correction of all existing evils."

Because neither Stanton nor Anthony had ever endured factory work, they did not fully appreciate the hardships of the workplace. At a meeting to organize seamstresses into a cooperative, Anthony listened in horror to stories about the women's long hours and pitiful wages. But the advice she gave them in her remarks was useless: "You must not work for these stingy prices any longer. Have a spirit of independence...and you will get better wages for yourself." She and Stanton offered no concrete solutions to the hardships of working women's lives except to vigorously denounce the oft-cited evil of sexual inequality. The WWA disbanded in 1869 because of members' disillusionment with the organization's lack of accomplishment.

In February 1869, Congress began considering adoption of the 15th Amendment. It declared that neither the federal government nor individual states could prohibit a U.S. citizen from voting "on account of race, color, or previous condition of servitude." It did not forbid states from using sex as a reason for barring citizens from voting and therefore did not promote or protect women's right to vote.

At this time, a new organization, headquartered in Boston, had emerged. Founded by a group that included Lucy Stone, Henry Blackwell, Louisa May Alcott, and Julia Ward Howe, author of the "Battle Hymn of the Republic," the New England Woman Suffrage Association (NEWSA) was the first major political group dedicated solely to achieving woman suffrage. To avoid angering important allies among Republican congressmen, NEWSA members were willing to postpone efforts to secure the ballot for women until black male suffrage was the law of the land. The New England group soon found ways to lobby for woman suffrage that did not interfere with passage of the 15th Amendment. Its members focused on achieving woman suffrage in Washington, D.C., and newly settled western territories that were not yet states and decided to work for a Constitutional amendment in the future.

Predictably, Stanton scoffed at this strategy, certain it would never lead to getting the ballot. Instead, she and Anthony were perfectly willing to anger the Republicans and their former abolitionist allies by insisting that any Constitutional amendment must include woman suffrage as well as black male suffrage. During February 1869, she and Anthony embarked on a two-month tour of the Midwest to recruit support among women. They attended state suffrage meetings in Ohio, Illinois, Wisconsin, and Missouri. Despite much enthusiastic support, Stanton and Anthony also encountered a great deal of resistance to their stand against the 15th Amendment. Many women who had been active members of volunteer soldiers' relief organizations during the Civil War were unwilling to oppose the Republican party.

Discouraged but not defeated, Stanton and Anthony returned to New York to adjust their strategy. Instead of lobbying against the 15th Amendment, they decided to support a 16th Amendment to legalize woman suffrage. Although Stanton insisted that she was upholding the rights of all women by calling for a special woman suffrage amendment, she was actually defending the rights of women like herself—white, educated, and affluent—who would be left politically powerless when men of lesser education and means gained the ballot. "American women of wealth, education, virtue and refinement," she warned in the April 29, 1869, issue of the *Revolution,* "if you do not wish the lower orders of Chinese, Africans, Germans and Irish, with their low ideas of womanhood to make laws for you and your daughters, ... to dictate not only the civil, but moral codes by which you shall be governed, awake to the danger of your present position and demand that woman, too, shall be represented in the government."

Stanton's racist, bombastic words angered her colleagues in the American Equal Rights Association, and undermined her hopes of uniting all AERA members behind a 16th Amendment. On the morning of May 12, the American Equal Rights Association convened at Steinway Hall in New York City. Stephen Foster, a leading abolitionist and member of the New England Woman Suffrage Association, began the meeting by demanding that Stanton resign because of her association with George Train. Stanton refused.

Stanton then proceeded to further inflame the meeting when she denounced the 15th Amendment as an act that would secure "'manhood suffrage' and [establish] an aristocracy of sex on this continent. ... Think of Patrick and Sambo and Hans and Yung Tung," Stanton said, alluding to the Irish, blacks, Germans, and Chinese whom she considered to be "lower orders" of humankind, "who do not know the difference between a monarchy and a republic, who cannot read the Declaration of Independence or Webster's spelling book, making laws for ... women of wealth and education. ... Shall American statesmen ... so amend their constitutions as to make their wives and mothers the political inferiors of unlettered and unwashed ditch-diggers, bootblacks, butchers and barbers, fresh from the slave plantations of the South?"

When she finished, Frederick Douglass rose from his chair to speak. Surveying the audience from the lectern, he tried to control his anger at her stinging words. First he recalled the friendship they had shared over the years and declared that "there is no name greater than that of Elizabeth Cady Stanton in the matter of woman's rights and equal rights." But to call black Americans "Sambo" or dismiss them as bootblacks and ditch diggers—that he could not abide.

Douglass eloquently explained why he thought blacks must urgently have the vote. "When women, because they are women, are hunted down through the cities of New York and New Orleans; when they are dragged from their houses and hung upon lampposts; when their children are torn from their arms and their brains dashed out upon the pavement; when they are objects of insult and outrage at every turn; when they are in danger of having their homes burnt down...then they will have an urgency to obtain the ballot equal to our own." After Douglass finished speaking, the convention deteriorated into a cross fire of accusations as each side—Stanton and Anthony and their supporters versus the Boston group represented by Lucy Stone and Henry Blackwell—hardened its positions for or against the 15th Amendment and a host of other issues.

Three days later, Stanton and Anthony hosted a reception for women delegates to the AERA convention at the Women's Bureau. With an overflowing crowd representing 19 states, the reception turned into a business meeting, and the delegates formed a new organization: the National Woman Suffrage Association (NWSA). The founders set forth their goals at once—to fight for a 16th Amendment to enfranchise women and to dedicate themselves to securing other rights for women in the workplace and in marriage. Like a soldier marching into battle, Stanton declared, "We are ready. We are prepared."

Stanton was elected president, her cousin Elizabeth Smith Miller was elected vice-president, and Anthony was chosen to lead the executive committee. Stanton relished the power and pulpit that the NWSA provided to express her vision of women's emancipation. As she had before the war, she served as the intellectual architect for women's rights, this time on behalf of the NWSA, fashioning the daring, innovative ideas for which the NWSA stood.

On November 24, 1869, six months after the NWSA was founded, Lucy Stone and others organized the American

Woman Suffrage Association (AWSA) in Cleveland, Ohio. Unlike the NWSA, the new group encouraged men to assume leadership positions and even elected as its president the powerful and popular minister, Henry Ward Beecher, brother of Harriet Beecher Stowe. The blustery Brooklyn, New York, minister skillfully took lead of AWSA, and Lucy Stone headed up the executive committee.

The members of the American Woman Suffrage Association, like their counterparts in the NWSA, committed themselves to securing women's right to vote. But they chose a different strategy: they focused on winning woman suffrage in each state instead of through a national law. Stanton fiercely opposed the AWSA's state-by-state approach to securing the ballot. "To leave [woman suffrage] to the States and the partial acts of Congress, is to defer indefinitely its settlement," she argued in the *Revolution*. AWSA, moreover, had only one goal: securing the ballot. The NWSA hoped to achieve broader reforms.

The American Woman Suffrage Association focused on the needs and interests of middle-class professional and married women, and did not question traditional ideas about women's lives, especially the idea that all women should aspire to marry and have children. But under the leadership of Stanton and Anthony, the National Woman Suffrage Association advocated new goals and social roles for women—such as acquiring more education or seeking a profession, and the freedom to end abusive or unhappy marriages—and continued to champion the concerns of working-class women.

Despite the AWSA's growing strength, Stanton and other members of the NWSA boldly developed a new strategy to secure women's right to vote: to declare that the 14th Amendment to the U.S. Constitution already granted them that right. The 14th Amendment stated in part that "all citizens born or naturalized in the United States...are citizens of the United States" and that "no state shall make or enforce any law which shall abridge" the privileges and rights of any citizen. Because women were citizens and because voting was a right of citizenship, argued Stanton, women already had the right to vote and merely had to exercise it.

Virginia Minor, president of the Missouri branch of the NWSA, and her husband, Francis Minor, a lawyer and ardent suffrage supporter, had first made this argument in October 1869 at a woman suffrage convention in St. Louis. The New Departure, as the argument came to be known, soon caught fire, and Stanton quickly embraced the idea. By 1871, hundreds of women around the country tried to register to vote under its banner.

Meanwhile, the *Revolution* was in deep, irreversible debt. Its small circulation and paltry advertising revenues could not keep up with mounting production costs, and after less than three years as journalists, Anthony and Stanton were forced to suspend publication. Anthony personally assumed full responsibility for the massive debt—$10,000 plus interest—while Stanton made no attempt to help.

Stanton found a new method for spreading her views—by becoming a lecturer on the lyceum circuit. Lyceum, or public hall, lecturing paid well and became an avenue of employment for many educated women, for whom interesting and well-paying jobs were not readily available. The work paid about $75 to $100 a night—more than twice what most working-class women made in a month—minus traveling expenses and fees to the booking agencies that arranged these tours.

Stanton signed up with a speakers' bureau in November 1869 and soon plunged into the life of a traveling lecturer. Now 54, she had grown stouter as the years passed. But her ample girth did not slow her down, and she maintained a punishing schedule, speaking in a different village every day, sleeping on the road, and enduring crude accommodations and flavorless meals. This new life kept her away from her children for months. Although she and her husband were accustomed to being apart for long stretches, her three younger children, especially Harriot, found these separations harder. To her daughters, Stanton tried to justify her absences as a way to create a better future for them. She once wrote Margaret, "I feel that I am doing an immense amount of good in rousing women to thought and inspiring them with new hope and self-respect, that I am making the path smoother for you and Hattie and all the other dear girls."

Despite the hardships of lyceum travel and the lonely separation from her children, Stanton relished the opportunity to promote women's rights, and especially to share her ideas on marriage, motherhood, and women's health with women. Wherever she had a spare afternoon, she made a point of talking to women alone, hoping, as she wrote her cousin Elizabeth Smith Miller, to put "radical thoughts" into their heads.

More and more, Stanton's closest ties were with women: Anthony, Mott, her own daughters, and her mother and sisters, who took great interest in her work. Yet things had begun to change between Stanton and Anthony. They were still close, but Anthony no longer treated Stanton with the same degree of deference she had shown in the early years of their partnership. She did not hesitate to express her differences with Stanton, and she maintained her own punishing schedule of women's rights work that seldom included Stanton. Stanton's frequent absences from NWSA business and the financial fiasco of the *Revolution*—including Stanton's unwillingness to help pay off the debt—had created a minor rift between the two friends.

In January 1872, Stanton presided over the fourth annual NWSA convention in Washington. By then, she and Anthony had found a new ally in Victoria Woodhull, a dashing and provocative journalist who had appeared before a congressional committee the year before to argue for women's constitutional right to vote. Born into a colorful, eccentric family, Woodhull and her sister, Tennessee Claflin, moved to New York City in 1868 and became Wall Street speculators. After making enough money to live in a style that suited their lavish tastes, they turned their prodigious energies to politics, and both women became persuasive and provocative speakers for women's rights. In their journal, *Woodhull & Claflin's Weekly,* which they established in 1870, they espoused their controversial beliefs in favor of dress reform, legalized prostitution, world government, and free love, a movement that challenged the power of organized religion and wanted to abolish legal marriage because it stifled the dictates of the heart.

For her outspokenness, Woodhull earned the dubious titles of "Mrs. Satan" and "Queen of Prostitutes." But beneath her flamboyance lay the legal acuity of a constitutional scholar. Like Virginia and Francis Minor, she argued that women's right to vote was part of the inalienable right of citizenship protected by the 14th Amendment to the U.S. Constitution. But unlike the Minors, who sought justice from the courts, Woodhull urged Congress to pass an act explicitly stating that the U.S. Constitution granted the ballot to all American citizens, including women.

At first neither Stanton nor Anthony cared about Woodhull's colorful past or eyebrow-raising conduct. "Victoria C. Woodhull stands before us today a grand, brave woman, radical alike in political, religious, and social principles," Stanton declared in an article. But Anthony soon became alarmed by Woodhull's attempts to form a new political party—the People's party—and seek the NWSA's endorsement for her candidacy in the 1872 Presidential election. In fact, she planned to turn the annual NWSA meeting in May 1872 into a nominating convention for her Presidential bid.

For a time, Stanton supported Woodhull's candidacy, but her enthusiasm cooled when Woodhull accused Anthony of spreading harmful lies about her sister, Tennessee, in an effort

to discredit Woodhull. While still quite active in the NWSA, Stanton began to think that her most effective contribution to women's rights lay in writing and lecturing on her own. Suffrage continued to be central to Stanton's vision of women's emancipation, but she continued to advocate liberalized divorce laws and a woman's right to birth control.

During the 1870s, Stanton's life fell into a pleasant pattern of traveling for part of the year and enjoying happy family occasions when she was home. Every January, usually right after the NWSA's annual meeting, she left for a five-month lecture tour and stayed in touch with her husband and children through correspondence. She returned to the house that she had bought with her inheritance in Tenafly, New Jersey, for a family reunion every summer. During these warm and balmy months, she occupied herself with her children's college graduations and weddings and with socializing with neighbors at teas, picnics, and other festivities. After revising her lectures and getting the youngest children off to school in the fall, she resumed her lecturing for three more months until Christmas.

Victoria Woodhull, here asserting her right to vote, was brilliant and controversial. She contributed valuable new ideas and a dash of drama to the women's rights movement, and Stanton exulted to Woodhull, "In declaring that women are already citizens and pointing the short way to freedom, you have inspired the strongest of us with new hope and enthusiasm."

As her children matured, Stanton greatly enjoyed their companionship. She shared books and enjoyed vigorous debates with them about their reading. Like any devoted parent, she never hesitated to give maternal advice. She wrote Harriot how pleased she was that the young woman was reading a book about politics "so that you and I can continue our political discussions next summer as we drive over the blue hills of New Jersey." She also urged Hattie not to get drawn into any of the "religious excitement" at Vassar, the college she was attending. Perhaps recalling her own dreadful girlhood experiences in revival meetings at Troy Seminary, she told Hattie, "I prefer to have you walk in the open air, sleep, or read Plato to listening to the prayers of sentimental girls and to the recounting of their morbid experiences."

In the summer of 1876, as the nation prepared to celebrate its 100th birthday, Stanton, Anthony, and other NWSA leaders planned to remind the country that one half of its citizens still did not enjoy the rights and privileges of democracy. The NWSA leaders had requested that they be included as representatives in the official celebration that was being held in Philadelphia, with at least one NWSA member from each state included in the NWSA delegation. Instead they were offered six invitations.

Stanton and Lucretia Mott were incensed by this rebuff. They refused to attend the gala Centennial celebration and instead chose to conduct an alternative Centennial convention. But Anthony was determined to present their Declaration of Rights at the official event. During the official ceremonies on the morning of July 4, Anthony and four other women stood up and interrupted the presiding officer. They presented him with their declaration, then gaily scattered copies of the declaration to eager spectators. Then they proceeded outside where Anthony read the Women's Declaration of Rights in front of the Liberty Bell.

As Anthony read the articles of impeachment, which Stanton had drafted, a crowd cheered her on. In unflinching language, the articles described the numerous violations of women's rights, such as taxation without representation; a harsher code of conduct for women than for men; and denial of the most fundamental right of all: the ballot. Anthony closed by declaring, "'We ask justice, we ask equality, we ask that all the civil and political rights that belong to citizens of the United States, be guaranteed to us and our daughters forever.'"

As the crowd cheered, Anthony intoned, "And for the violation of these fundamental principles of our government, we arraign our rulers on this Fourth day of July, 1876—and these are our articles of impeachment." To impeach, or accuse, the government of the United States of violating fundamental principles was very serious. It was a bold and courageous act by women who wanted to hold their leaders accountable for violating their rights.

Newspapers across the country carried notices about Anthony's surprise presentation of the Declaration of Rights at the Centennial celebration. Not surprisingly, the *New York Tribune* assailed Anthony's act as a "very discourteous interruption" and warned that it "prefigures new forms of violence and disregard of order which may accompany the participation of women in active partisan politics." The *St. Louis Dispatch* was more charitable and amusingly suggested that, along with their declaration, women should take up arms to demand suffrage. "[I]f General Susan B. Anthony, in command of a bloomer regiment, should march into the halls of congress...and demand the passage of a law in behalf of woman suffrage," no man would dare refuse them.

Pleased by the publicity and attention their Centennial protest aroused, Stanton, Anthony, and other NWSA leaders decided to focus on lobbying for a 16th Amendment to the U.S. Constitution that would give women the right to vote. The New Departure approach was not working. The final blow to New Departure had come the year before, in 1875, when the U.S. Supreme Court ruled against Virginia Minor, who had tried to vote in the 1872 Presidential election.

On January 11 and 12, 1878, Stanton and several other NWSA members testified before a Senate committee on behalf of a 16th Amendment. After the other women spoke, Stanton delivered a brilliant legal analysis of the U.S. Constitution, insisting that it already gave women electoral power. "This is declared to be a government 'of the people.' All power, it is said, centers in the people.... When we say people, do we not mean women as well as men?" Like a lawyer arguing before a judge, she cited court cases that upheld women's constitutional right to vote. She quoted from the Founding Fathers, reviewed constitutional history, and analyzed recent political events; she spoke urgently but incisively, marshaling evidence with precision and eloquence. While she spoke, the chairman of the committee, Senator Benjamin Wadleigh of New Hampshire, deliberately ignored her. He read a newspaper, shuffled papers, cut his nails, sharpened a pencil, stretched, yawned, and gazed up at the ceiling. Enraged, Stanton had to restrain herself from hurling her speech at him. Not surprisingly, a few months later, Senator Wadleigh reported back to the Senate that the

During the 1870s, Stanton and her allies repeatedly testified before Congress that the U.S. Constitution already granted women the right to vote. At a Senate hearing in January 1872, she boldly declared: "You may consider me presumptuous, gentlemen, but I claim to be a citizen of the United States, with all the qualifications of a voter."

committee did not endorse a 16th Amendment, calling it "an experiment so novel, a change so great."

Discouraged but undaunted, Stanton and Anthony organized a convention in Anthony's hometown of Rochester, New York, in July 1878 to celebrate the 30th anniversary of the Seneca Falls Convention. Stanton valiantly cheered her coactivists on. "To those of you on this platform who for these 30 years have been the steadfast representatives of woman's cause, my friends and co-laborers, let me say our work has not been in vain. True, we have not yet secured the suffrage; but we have aroused public thought to the many disabilities of our sex, and our countrywomen to higher self-respect and worthier ambition, and in this struggle for justice we have deepened and broadened our own lives and extended the horizon of our vision."

By the end of the decade, Stanton was looking for new ways to expand her vision of women's lives while reexamining her own life. After an accident in which the horse-drawn vehicle that she was traveling in overturned and left her limping in pain for several weeks, followed by a bout of pneumonia, she decided to give up the lyceum circuit altogether. On March 26, 1879, she wrote despairingly to Elizabeth Smith Miller from Joplin, Missouri, "I have been wandering, wandering...sleepy and disgusted with my profession, as there is no rest from the time the season begins until it ends.... [I] must...eat 183 more miserable meals... smile, try to look intelligent and interested in everyone who approaches me, while I feel like a squeezed sponge."

It was time now to turn her sights to other goals and strategies for winning women's emancipation.

Old age and philosophical differences did not slow down Stanton and Anthony's quest for female equality or weaken their close, long-standing friendship. Stanton wrote in her autobiography, "In thought and sympathy we were one, and in the division of labor we exactly complemented each other."

8

"I GET MORE RADICAL AS I GROW OLDER"

On November 12, 1880, Stanton celebrated her 65th birthday by starting a diary. "Today I am sixty-five years old, am perfectly well, am a moderate eater, sleep well and am generally happy. My philosophy is to live one day at a time; neither to waste my forces in apprehension of evils to come, nor regrets for the blunders of the past."

A few days before, she had tried to vote for the first time in her life. Anthony, who had been arrested and fined for voting unlawfully in the 1872 Presidential election, accompanied her to the polls. When they approached the ballot box, one of the poll inspectors seized it and exclaimed, "Oh, no, madam! Men only are allowed to vote."

Stanton explained that women had voted until 1807, when an "arbitrary" act of the state legislature prohibited them from doing so, and she insisted that, as a tax-paying citizen of the United States, she had a right to vote. Stanton briskly informed the inspectors that she wished to cast her vote "as a citizen of the United States." But the inspector held on to the ballot box and would not allow her to drop her ballot into it. So, as she recounted in her autobiography, "I laid my ballot in his hand, saying that I had the same right to vote that any man present had, and on him must rest the responsibility of denying me my rights of citizenship." Proudly, she wrote to her children Theodore and Harriot, "The whole town is agape with my act."

Another momentous event had occurred in November—the death of Lucretia Mott, on November 11, the day before Stanton's birthday. In her diary, Stanton recorded her sadness about the death of her dear friend and vowed to "imitate her noble example." Mott's death inspired Stanton and Anthony to get to work on a project they had long envisioned—a history of the women's rights movement, which Mott had first suggested. Anthony shipped several trunks and boxes containing an accumulation of more than 30 years of documents and artifacts from her home in Rochester to Stanton's country home. In late November she moved in with Stanton to begin the daunting task of crafting a coherent book.

They completed the first volume in six months, an opus of 878 pages that brought the movement up to 1860. Stanton and Anthony took the summer off from research and writing to travel through New England and recruit new members for the NWSA. At the end of July 1881, Stanton wrote a letter to Anthony prodding her to "leave these state conventions alone...at least until we can finish the History." By the end of October, Stanton reported in her diary, they were back in Tenafly, deep "in the toils of another thousand-paged volume." Anthony, in an uncharacteristic attack of despair, described their labors in her diary as "a wilderness of work, a swamp of letters and papers almost hopeless."

By the end of 1881, they finished volume 2, which covered 1861 to 1876. Harriot, who had returned home from her studies abroad to help them with the writing, urged her mother to travel to France with her, and the two women set sail a short time later. After almost two years of unrelenting work on the *History,* Stanton, as she recalled in her autobiography, was eager to escape across the ocean "beyond the reach and sound of my beloved Susan and the woman suffrage movement."

After a fairly smooth crossing, Stanton and her daughter stayed with her son Theodore and his French wife at their home near Jacournassy, in the south of France. There, Stanton met her first grandchild, Elizabeth Cady Stanton II, or Lizette, and helped Theodore put together *The Woman Question in Europe*. In July, she and Harriot traveled to Toulouse, France, where Hattie enrolled at the university to study for a master's degree in mathematics, because no American university accepted women for graduate work.

For Stanton this was the first of several trips she would make to Europe over the next few years. She had not been back to Europe since her honeymoon 42 years before. In Toulouse, she and Harriot stayed at a Catholic convent and she quickly settled into a leisurely routine of reading, walking in the garden, and writing letters. "These were days, for me, of perfect rest and peace," she recalled in her autobiography. "Everything moved as if by magic, no hurry and bustle. . . . As only one or two of the sisters spoke English, I could read under the trees uninterruptedly for hours. Emerson, Ruskin, and Carlyle were my chosen companions."

From France, Stanton went to England and traveled throughout that country. Meanwhile, Anthony had arrived in London, and she and Stanton lectured on the American suffrage movement and met with British suffragists. On September 30, 1883, Stanton had reason to rejoice; Hattie, who had married William Henry Blatch, an Englishman she had met on an earlier ocean crossing, gave birth to her first child, Nora. Stanton savored this special time with her daughter and infant granddaughter. "As I sit here beside Hattie with the baby in my arms," she happily wrote in her diary, "and realize that three generations of us are together, I appreciate more than ever what each generation can do for the next one, by making the most of itself."

She left a month later, ready to go back home and resume her work on the *History*. Saying good-bye to Hattie was very hard. Silently, they held hands and gazed into each other's eyes, each imprinting the image of the other in memory. Stanton did not cry, but her legs "trembled so that I could scarcely walk to the carriage." She rejoined Anthony, and they sailed to New York. "Unspeakably happy" to be back home, Stanton embarked on a round of visits to family and friends, and settled into her family home in Johnstown because she had rented out her house in Tenafly.

In May 1884, Stanton had returned to her home in Tenafly and Anthony arrived armed with "a number of appalling boxes of papers," and they set to work on volume 3 of the *History*. The two old friends enjoyed long days of work and companionship. "Susan and I take moonlight walks now and then. When weary, we sit on the benches which I have had scattered along the hillside road, and we gaze at the moon." Stanton liked to pick out constellations. Describing one "bewitching" moonlit night in her diary, she wrote that Orion looked "stretched out like a great lion."

Meanwhile, Stanton also worked on other writing projects and enjoyed visits from her husband. Although Henry continued to live and practice law in New York City, he spent more time with his wife in Tenafly. As their children married and started families of their own, the elder Stantons drew closer together to share these happy family events. In these later years of their marriage, the Stantons found a balance between companionship and the freedom to pursue their own interests. "Henry drove over to Ridgewood the other evening to fetch me back," Stanton recorded in her diary one crisp October evening in 1885, "and we had a lovely return in the twilight."

But Stanton's contentment with life was soon to be cruelly disrupted. In October 1886, Stanton sailed for England with Hattie, little Nora, and a nanny. She had been in England for almost two months when, on January 14, 1887, Hattie appeared at her door, ashen faced and clutching a telegram from the States. Henry had died suddenly from pneumonia. Stanton was stunned. "Death!" she wrote in her diary. "We all think we are prepared to hear of the passing away of the aged. But when the news comes, the heart and pulses all seem to stand still. . . . I have lived with my husband forty-six years, and now he leads the way to another sphere." She and Hattie sat together the rest of the day talking "of the mysteries of life and death."

Henry's death did not greatly change Stanton's life. After all, she had lived on her own, traveled as she pleased, and earned and managed her own money for many years. She was 72 when her husband died. Still in good health but increasingly slowed down by obesity, she was mentally sharp as ever, full of plans and writing projects and eager to return to the fracas of women's rights.

In March 1888, she gave the keynote address at the first international women's rights convention in Washington, D.C. This event was the brainchild of Stanton and Anthony, an idea they had developed during their European tour of 1883. Delegates from France, England, Ireland, Italy, Norway, Finland, Canada, and even India attended, as well

In 1888, Stanton and Anthony organized a meeting of women's rights advocates from around the globe. At the international convention, held in Washington, D.C., Stanton told the delegates, "Our gathering here to-day is highly significant.... When, in the history of the world, was there ever before such an assemblage of able, educated women?"

as representatives from more than 50 American women's organizations. Although most of the delegates were white middle- and upper-class women, some of the speakers were not. Huldah Loud, head of the Women's Department of the Knights of Labor, a major union composed of factory workers, farmers, and small business owners, addressed the gathering, as did Frances Ellen Harper, a well-known African-American reformer and lecturer. And, most astonishing of all, Lucy Stone—who had not shared the same podium with Stanton and Anthony in almost 20 years—and other members of the rival American Woman Suffrage Association were there.

Though she was pleased by the success of the International Council, Stanton was alarmed by Anthony's desire to work only for suffrage and ignore other women's rights goals. She was especially dismayed by her old friend's eagerness to make suffrage a respectable cause in order to gain more public support. Stanton feared that Anthony's attempts to win support from religious and other socially traditional groups would dilute the bold, expansive vision of the

NWSA. She urged Anthony to use the original Declaration of Sentiments from the 1848 Seneca Falls Convention. "I tell her that I get more radical as I grow older," Stanton wrote in her diary, "while she seems to get more conservative."

In February 1890, the National Woman Suffrage Association and the American Woman Suffrage Association finally buried their old resentments and merged into the National American Woman Suffrage Association (NAWSA). Both Stanton and Anthony were nominated for the office of president, but Stanton won by 41 votes. Anthony was elected vice president at large, and Lucy Stone was chosen to serve as head of the executive committee. The delegates had high hopes that through NAWSA they would quickly achieve their main goal: the right to vote.

But, as ever, Stanton was loath to focus only on achieving woman suffrage. In her address to the founding convention of NAWSA, Stanton laid out her broad, expansive vision for the new organization. "We must manifest a broad catholic spirit for all shades of opinion in which we may differ and recognize the equal rights of all parties, sects and races, tribes and colors," she exhorted the delegates. "Colored women, Indian women, Mormon women and women from every quarter of the globe have been heard in these Washington conventions and I trust they always will be."

Almost instantly, Stanton ran afoul of younger NAWSA leaders who had no interest in pursuing her ambitious goals. They were just as happy to see her go off to England and let Anthony, whose single-minded goal of getting the vote suited their purposes, serve as acting president.

Stanton returned to England shortly after the convention and enjoyed a round of visits with English suffragists. But once again, personal tragedy intruded on these happy times with her daughter and her granddaughter. In January 1891, her oldest son, Daniel, died unexpectedly, and her sister Tryphena passed away that May. Abruptly, she returned home in August 1891.

During the 18 months that she had been gone, Anthony had kept her up to date on NAWSA's activities, and Stanton had sent speeches for Anthony to read at NAWSA meetings. Now that Stanton was back in the United States, Anthony urged her to attend the 1892 convention in Washington, D.C. Stanton begged off at first, claiming that her children wanted her to rest, but Anthony dismissed that and personally escorted her to the convention.

There, on January 18, 1892, Stanton gave perhaps the most masterful speech of her life. "The Solitude of Self," as the speech came to be called, was both a clarion call for equal political rights and a poetic meditation on the ultimate solitude and loneliness that every person faces in life. "The strongest reason why we ask for woman a voice in the government under which she lives; in the religion she is asked to believe; equality in social life, where she is the chief factor; a place in the trades and professions, where she may earn her bread, is because...as an individual, she must rely on herself.... The talk of sheltering woman from the fierce storms of life is the sheerest mockery, for they beat on her from every point of the compass, just as they do on man, and with more fatal results, for he has been trained to protect himself, to resist, and to conquer." Each person, Stanton continued, has an inner essence—a "solitude of self"—that no other human being can fully comprehend or deign to control. The speech embodied Stanton's uncompromising view that women must learn to be responsible for themselves—to throw off their dependence upon men and live their lives as self-reliant human beings. Eloquent and stirring, the "Solitude of Self" speech was the sublime result of Stanton's many years of reflection upon women's lives.

With that, she stepped down as NAWSA president, hoping to be done with all organizational work. Stanton continued to write speeches for Anthony to deliver at NAWSA meetings and other events. She also wrote articles on women's rights and other issues for current-events magazines such as the *Arena,* the *Nation,* and the *North American Review.* In the April 1894 issue of the *Arena,* she wrote about one of her chief goals, divorce reform, and declared, "The question of divorce, like marriage, should be settled, as to its most sacred relations, by the parties themselves; neither the State nor the Church having any right to intermeddle therein." In another article, she advocated a five-day workweek.

On November 12, 1895, Stanton was honored at an 80th birthday celebration attended by 6,000 well-wishers at New York's Metropolitan Opera House. For three hours, she listened to lavish tributes by representatives of suffrage groups from across the nation and Europe. She heard poems recited in her honor and was thrilled by a choral performance by a group of African-American children. She was especially touched by the gift of a silver and onyx ballot box from a group of Mormon women in Utah, who had already received the right to vote. The box could not be opened, a poignant reminder that eastern women still lacked that most basic democratic right.

But, in her usual manner, she soon set tongues wagging in disapproval again. Two weeks after her 80th birthday celebration, the first volume of Stanton's two-volume critique of the Bible, *The Woman's Bible,* was published (the second volume was published in 1898). As the book made its way into readers' hands and reviewers' columns, Stanton once again aroused public fury. Alarmed by what she viewed as a creeping penetration of religious ideology into the nation's social and political life, even into the women's rights movement, Stanton had first started working on a study of the Old and New Testaments during the 1880s. In writing *The Woman's Bible,* Stanton had two goals. The first was to demonstrate that, far from being the inviolable word of God, the Bible was the product of male authors who mostly believed that women were inferior in all respects to men. She also wanted to show that religious authorities—notably male clergy—had misread or misinterpreted neutral biblical views of women in order to argue for women's social and moral inferiority.

Stanton divided her study into two parts, and focused only on those sections of the Old and New Testaments that referred to women or, in her opinion, should have included them. She quoted from Scripture first and then presented her commentary below. She argued in a concise, lawyerly manner, relying on a careful, critical reading of each biblical passage. For example, contrary to the popular scriptural interpretation that God created man first and woman as an afterthought—therefore making her subject to man's authority—she demonstrated how a careful reading of Scripture shows that God created both sexes simultaneously in the image of God.

Stanton also turned popular conceptions of Eve on their head. Rather than being an evil temptress who corrupts the innocent Adam with the poison of knowledge, Stanton argued, Eve sought a more meaningful life beyond "picking flowers and talking with Adam, [which] did not satisfy." Stanton declared that the unbiased reader must be "impressed with the courage, the dignity, and the lofty ambition of the woman. The tempter...did not try to tempt her...by brilliant jewels, rich dresses, worldly luxuries or pleasures, but with the promise of knowledge, with the wisdom of the gods." Stanton's analysis was original and thought-provoking.

Volume 1 went through seven printings in just six months and was translated into several foreign languages. It won acclaim from Stanton's supporters and condemnation from her opponents. Not surprisingly, *The Woman's Bible* upset many delegates in the increasingly conservative NAWSA. In January 1896, delegates at the NAWSA's annual convention began to draft a resolution of censure against Stanton. Though Anthony had vigorously disassociated herself from *The Woman's Bible,* she eloquently defended her long-standing partner and friend at the convention. In spite of Anthony's defense, the resolution passed by a vote of 53 to 41. The censure hurt Stanton, but she decided not to resign from NAWSA. Angrily, she penned a rebuttal to the censure, declaring that she would continue to "lift women out of all these dangerous and degrading [religious] superstitions."

While Anthony rushed breathlessly from one event and meeting to another, Stanton was content to remain at her home in New York City to think and write. By 1896, her eyesight had started to fail and she was very distressed at the prospect of going blind. Although she could still write without wearing spectacles, she could not read her own writing. She kept up a steady output of articles and, in 1898, published her autobiography, *Eighty Years and More,* a chatty public record of her life.

As long as she could write and convey her ideas, Stanton felt a thirst for life. "I must confess that I am in no hurry to [die]. Life has been, and still is, very sweet to me, and there are many things I desire to do before I take final leave of this planet." She continued to refine her ideas about social reform and lamented how narrow and conservative her fellow reformers had become by focusing only on suffrage. Increasingly interested in the ideas and theories of socialism, an international political movement to abolish capitalism and replace it with a more equitable and humane economic system, she continually badgered the NAWSA to broaden its concerns. She vented her frustration in her diary, writing on May 10, 1898, "The longer I live, the more I am struck with the stupidity of people in not doing the right thing at the right time. Our younger coadjutors seem to be too satisfied with painting in the brightest colors the successes of the woman movement, while leaving in the background the long line of wrongs which we still deplore. . . . But when the vast majority of us are deprived of all of our civil and political rights, the struggle must be a fierce one."

text continues on page 124

"BOYS ARE CHEAPER THAN MACHINERY": STANTON'S OUTRAGE OVER CHILD LABOR

In her last years, Stanton continued to pursue a wide-ranging agenda of social change. In this letter to Susan B. Anthony, she angrily condemns Americans' concerns over the Spanish-American War, in which the United States clashed with Spain over the latter's aggression against Cuba and the Philippines. Stanton was outraged that Americans were more concerned about the horrors of war and the welfare of American soldiers in a faraway conflict than about the horrors of child labor at home. Stanton used the formal salutation "My Dear Miss Anthony" because she intended for Anthony to present the letter at the 50th anniversary Woman Suffrage Convention in Rochester, New York.

New York
April 27, 1898

My Dear Miss Anthony:

You ask me to send a letter as to woman's position in regard to the war. Many with whom I talk feel aggrieved that they have no voice in declaring war with Spain, or in protesting against it. The vast majority of men are in the same position. Why care for a voice in an event that may happen once in a lifetime, more than in those of far greater importance continually before us? Why groan over the horrors of war, when the tragedies of peace are forever before us? Our boys in blue, well fed and clothed in camp and hospital, are better off than our boys in rags, overworked in mines, in factories, in prison houses, and in bare, dingy dwellings called homes where the family meet at scanty meals after working ten hours, to talk over their hopeless situation in the despair of poverty.

A friend of mine visited the bleaching department in one of our New England factories, where naked boys, oiled from head to foot, are used to tramp pieces of shirting in a large vat. The chemicals necessary for bleaching are so strong as to eat the skin unless well oiled. In time they affect the eyes and lungs. There these boys, in relays, tramp, tramp all day, but not to music nor inspired with the love of country. In England they have machinery for such work; but in the land of the Puritans, boys are cheaper than machinery.

On the platform of one idea mothers cannot discuss these wrongs. We may talk of the cruelties in Cuba now on any platform, but not of the outrages of rich manufacturers in the State of Massachusetts. . . .

Elizabeth Cady Stanton

Despite their political and strategic differences, Stanton and Anthony remained warm friends. Because Anthony traveled so much, they seldom saw each other. Anthony still came for visits, but she no longer stayed with Stanton for long stretches of time. For Anthony's 80th birthday on February 15, 1900, Stanton penned a poetic tribute to her that began:

> My honored friend, I'll ne'er forget,
> That day in June, when first we met;
> Oh! would I had the skill to paint,
> My vision, of that "Quaker Saint."

But Stanton was also jealous of the love and respect lavished on Anthony by younger suffragists. "They have given Susan thousands of dollars, jewels, laces, silks and satins, and me, criticisms and denunciations for my radical ideas," she wrote plaintively to a friend in 1901.

In spite of her protests about wanting the NAWSA to be as inclusive as possible, by 1902 Stanton seemed to be having second thoughts about expanding the number of voters. For the annual convention in 1902, Stanton, as in the past, sent Susan Anthony a proposed topic to bring up at the meeting: "Educated Suffrage." In her letter to Anthony Stanton declared that only men and women who could "read and write the English language intelligently" should be allowed to vote. "[I]t seems very unwise to give all classes of humanity, the vicious as well as the virtuous, the ignorant as well as the learned, every foreigner landing on our shores, a voice in the government, of which they have no knowledge." Stanton was reacting to the massive influx of immigrants from Central and Eastern Europe who had begun arriving in America in the early 1880s to escape religious persecution or to seek better economic opportunities. Even her daughter Harriot, now quite active in the suffrage movement, was appalled at her mother's elitist attitude.

By 1902, Stanton could look back to see the fruits of 50 years of agitation for women's rights. Women were attending college and entering the professions, and married women had gained greater control of their property and more personal independence. In some western states, women even had the ballot. And though Stanton lamented the narrow goals of NAWSA, it was part of a broad and powerful international women's rights movement that she had helped to spark. Stanton's constant stirring up, born of a brilliant and uncompromising vision of women's equality, had indeed spawned greater public awareness and tangible accomplishments for women.

Nor did she stop stirring up even now as her eyesight dimmed and her strength diminished. On October 25, she dictated a draft of a letter to President Theodore Roosevelt, urging him to work for a woman suffrage amendment. She shrewdly reminded him that he was in favor of using the power of the federal government to curb the growth of corporate monopolies. Then she declared, "Surely, there is no greater monopoly than that of all men in denying to all women a voice in the laws they are compelled to obey."

Stanton had been suffering from shortness of breath for some time now and, according to Harriot, had urged her doctor to give her "something to send me packhorse speed to heaven" if he could not cure her condition. On Sunday morning, October 26, 1902, she instructed her housekeeper to fix up her hair in the halo of small curls she favored, and then she wanted to get dressed. But Harriot dissuaded her because she seemed so tired. Garbed in a dressing gown, Stanton stood with assistance, resting her hands on a table in front of her. Mustering up all of her energy, she drew herself very erect and stood at attention for several minutes, gazing proudly before her. She stood as she had stood so many times before. Perhaps she was silently reciting one of the hundreds of speeches she had made about women's rights. Then, at her daughter's urging, she sat down and promptly fell asleep. Two hours later, her nurse and Harriot moved her to her bed, and Stanton quietly died in her sleep.

Buttons, ribbons, and other memorabilia helped to commemorate special conventions and anniversaries of both the American Woman Suffrage Association and the National Woman Suffrage Association. The ribbon on the left fittingly includes pictures of Lucretia Mott (top) and Stanton (bottom). The ribbon on the right commemorates the 60th anniversary of the Seneca Falls convention and includes the motto "Votes for Women."

Anthony was overcome by grief. "I am too crushed to say much," she told reporters. "If I had died first she would have found beautiful phrases to describe our friendship, but I cannot put it into words." On her way to the funeral, she penned a letter to a friend, "Well, it is an awful hush—it seems impossible—that the voice is hushed that I longed to hear for fifty years—longed to get her opinion of things—before I knew exactly where I stood."

As Stanton had wished, the funeral was simple, a private service conducted in her New York City apartment. Moncure

Conway, an old friend, officiated, and the Reverend Antoinette Brown Blackwell gave one of the eulogies. Then Stanton's casket was transported out of the apartment and to the quiet, tree-shaded Woodlawn Cemetery in the Bronx, New York. The Reverend Phebe Hanaford, a contributor to *The Woman's Bible,* led the graveside service. And Elizabeth Cady Stanton, the incomparable champion of women's emancipation, was laid to rest.

Epilogue

American women finally achieved the right to vote in 1920, almost two decades after Elizabeth Cady Stanton died. Like Stanton, Susan B. Anthony did not live to see the passage of the amendment that granted women that right, though it is named after her—the Susan B. Anthony Amendment. She died nearly four years after Stanton, on March 13, 1906.

The NAWSA continued its efforts on behalf of women's causes, including suffrage, after Stanton's death. Its leaders followed a long-standing policy of working for woman suffrage within each state, an inefficient approach for winning suffrage for all American women.

In the early part of the 20th century, several new woman suffrage organizations emerged. The Boston Equal Suffrage Association for Good Government and the College Equal Suffrage League attracted younger women who introduced bold new methods for spreading their message, such as going door to door in city and suburban neighborhoods and organizing open-air meetings. In 1907, Stanton's daughter, Harriot Stanton Blatch, organized the Equality League of Self-Supporting Women, an alliance of middle- and upper-class professional women and working-class women from factories, laundries, and garment shops in New York City. Blatch and other activists hoped to take suffrage out of the parlor and into the street, to replace respectability with publicity. They organized outdoor meetings to draw publicity

Stanton's daughter Harriot Stanton Blatch, in the back seat, and granddaughter Nora Blatch de Forest, behind the wheel, proudly take the struggle for woman suffrage to the streets of New York City in 1908. The banner spread over the hood of the car reads: "Votes for Women."

and more converts, grand parades down Fifth Avenue in New York City, and well-publicized trolley-car campaigns.

In 1912, Alice Paul and Lucy Burns, two young suffragists who had participated in the militant wing of the British woman suffrage movement, organized the Congressional Union, a new branch of NAWSA. This group reorganized as the National Woman's party (NWP) in 1916. NWP members picketed the White House the following year to protest President Woodrow Wilson's opposition to a constitutional amendment. Starting in 1917, they picketed every day, holding signs that read: "Mr. President, What Will You Do for Woman Suffrage?"

At first, tourists and even the police officers dispatched to keep an eye on them supported their cause, but when the United States entered World War I on April 6, 1917, public support soon turned into public hostility. The picketers were arrested on the flimsy charge of obstructing traffic on city sidewalks. Found guilty, Alice Paul and 96 other suffragists were thrown into jail, where for six months and more they endured intolerable conditions: physical abuse by guards; fetid, airless cells; spoiled, worm-ridden food; and solitary confinement. When they went on a hunger strike to protest their treatment, prison officials jammed tubes down their throats and force-fed them.

This 1895 photograph of Stanton and Anthony served as the model for the statue of them and Lucretia Mott, which now stands in the United States Capitol. In this photo, Miss Thompson (center) stands in for Mott, who died in 1880. Stanton's daughter Margaret is seated in the bottom right.

By the time World War I ended on November 11, 1918, American women could vote in 16 states: Wyoming, Utah, Colorado, Idaho, Kansas, Oregon, Montana, Nevada, North Dakota, Ohio, Indiana, Nebraska, Arkansas, Michigan, Rhode Island, and New York. But the other 32 states still prohibited women from voting in state or national elections.

After being defeated in Congress in 1918 by only two votes, the 19th Amendment made it successfully through the House of Representatives on May 21, 1919. Just two weeks later, on June 4, 1919, the Senate also passed the amendment and sent it on to the states for ratification. Finally, on August 26, 1920, woman suffrage became the law of the land. A few days earlier, Harry Burns, a 24-year-old state representative from Tennessee, had cast the deciding vote on orders from his prosuffrage mother to support the Susan B. Anthony Amendment. His vote made Tennessee the 36th and final state needed to ratify the amendment. It had been 72 years since Elizabeth Cady Stanton, nervous but determined, had stood in front of a gathering of women and men in Seneca Falls, New York, and had demanded that most basic right of American citizenship.

CHRONOLOGY

November 12, 1815
Elizabeth Cady is born in Johnstown, New York

1831
Graduates from Johnstown Academy

1833
Graduates from Troy Female Seminary

May 1, 1840
Marries Henry Stanton; on May 12 they set sail for London to attend the World's Anti-Slavery Convention

March 2, 1842
Gives birth to her first child, Daniel Cady Stanton

March 15, 1844
Her second child, Henry B. Stanton, is born; the Stantons move to Boston shortly after

September 18, 1845
Gives birth to her third child, Gerrit Smith Stanton

October 1847
The Stantons move to Seneca Falls, New York

1848
Married Woman's Property Act is passed by the New York State legislature

July 19–20, 1848
The first women's rights convention in the United States takes place in Seneca Falls

February 9, 1851
Gives birth to her fourth child, Theodore Weld Stanton

May 1851
Meets Susan B. Anthony

April 1852
Elected president of the Women's New York State Temperance Society, her first elected leadership position

October 20, 1852
Gives birth to her fifth child and first daughter, Margaret Livingston Stanton

February 14, 1854
Delivers a speech to the New York State Woman's Rights Convention advocating expansion of the Married Woman's Property Act

January 20, 1856
Gives birth to her sixth child, Harriot Eaton Stanton

March 13, 1859
Gives birth to her seventh and last child, Robert Livingston Stanton

March 15, 1860
The New York State legislature passes an expanded Married Woman's Property Act

April 12, 1861
The Civil War begins

August 1861
The Stantons move to New York City

May 14, 1863
Stanton and Anthony organize the Women's Loyal National League

April 9, 1865
The Civil War ends

May 1866
The American Equal Rights Association is formed; Lucretia Mott is president, and Stanton is first vice president

June 13, 1866
The 14th Amendment is passed; grants African-American men the right to vote but does not extend the right to women

October 1866
Stanton runs for Congress as an independent candidate from New York City; she is the first woman to run for Congress

September 1867
Stanton and Anthony embark on a campaign throughout Kansas on behalf of both woman and black male suffrage

January 8, 1868
The first issue of the *Revolution* appears

September 16, 1868
Stanton and Anthony help establish the Working Woman's Association (WWA)

May 15, 1869
Stanton and Anthony establish the National Woman Suffrage Association (NWSA)

November 1869
Stanton launches her career as a lyceum speaker

November 24, 1869
Lucy Stone and her allies form the American Woman Suffrage Association (AWSA)

May 1870
The *Revolution* ceases publication under Stanton and Anthony

July 4, 1876
Stanton, Anthony, and their allies distribute a Declaration of Rights at the Centennial celebration in Philadelphia

1881
Stanton and Anthony publish the first two volumes of *History of Woman Suffrage*

1886
They publish the third volume of *History of Woman Suffrage*

January 14, 1887
Henry Stanton dies while Stanton is in Europe

March 1888
Stanton and Anthony host the first international women's rights convention in Washington, D.C.

February 1890
The National American Woman Suffrage Association (NAWSA) is formed out of the NWSA and the AWSA

January 18, 1892
Delivers her masterful speech "The Solitude of Self"

November 12, 1895
Tribute to Stanton held at the Metropolitan Opera House in New York City

November 1895
Publishes the first volume of *The Woman's Bible*

1898
Publishes her autobiography, *Eighty Years and More*, and the second volume of *The Woman's Bible*

October 26, 1902
Stanton dies

March 13, 1906
Anthony dies

August 26, 1920
The 19th Amendment is ratified; American women finally gain the right to vote

MUSEUMS AND HISTORIC SITES

Elizabeth Cady Stanton Home
32 Washington Street
Seneca Falls, NY 13148
315-568-2991

Built in 1836, this house is now part of the Women's Rights National Historic Park (see below). The house contains Stanton's piano, china service, and a few pieces of furniture, along with reproductions of the wallpaper she chose when she had the house renovated.

Women's Rights National Historical Park
136 Fall Street
Seneca Falls, NY 13148
315-568-2991
www.nps.gov/wori

This park commemorates the site of the Seneca Falls women's rights convention and includes an exhibition hall and multimedia theater. Next to the Visitor Center is the site of the Wesleyan Chapel, where the convention was held. Parts of the original building are still standing, and one wall is inscribed with the Declaration of Sentiments.

The Suffrage Monument (statue)
U.S. Capitol Building
Washington, DC
www.aoc.gov/cc/art/rotunda/suffrage_1.htm

This eight-ton marble statue of Elizabeth Cady Stanton, Susan B. Anthony, and Lucretia Mott is located in the Capitol's main Rotunda and was dedicated on February 15, 1921, Anthony's birthday. The statue, by sculptor Adelaide Johnson, has attracted the same kind of controversy and ridicule that its subjects endured during their lifetimes. One senator said, "The impression it makes is that the subjects are buried alive," and tour guides have jokingly referred to the statue as the "ladies in the bathtub."

Susan B. Anthony House
17 Madison Street
Rochester, NY 14608
716-235-6124
www.susanbanthonyhouse.org

This three-story red brick structure is now a museum filled with photographs and documents pertaining to the organized women's rights movement, along with Anthony's furniture and personal belongings. The web site offers a virtual tour of the house and links to other women's history sites and resources.

FURTHER READING

WRITINGS OF ELIZABETH CADY STANTON

Eighty Years and More: Reminiscences 1815–1897. 1898. Reprint, New York: Schocken, 1971.

Elizabeth Cady Stanton: As Revealed in Her Letters, Diary and Reminiscences. Edited by Theodore Stanton and Harriot Stanton Blatch. 2 vols. 1922. Reprint, New York: Arno and The New York Times, 1969.

The Elizabeth Cady Stanton–Susan B. Anthony Reader: Correspondence, Writings, Speeches. Edited by Ellen Carol DuBois. Revised edition, Boston: Northeastern University Press, 1992.

History of Woman Suffrage. Edited by Elizabeth Cady Stanton and Susan B. Anthony et al. 6 vols. 1881–1922. Reprint, Salem, N.H.: Ayer, 1985.

The Papers of Elizabeth Cady Stanton and Susan B. Anthony. Edited by Patricia G. Holland and Ann D. Gordon. Wilmington, Del.: Scholarly Resources, 1991. (Available in a microfilm edition of 45 reels, this collection reproduces all the letters, articles, essays, speeches, books, and other documents written by Stanton and Anthony.)

The Selected Papers of Elizabeth Cady Stanton and Susan B. Anthony. Vol. 1, *In the School of Anti-Slavery, 1840–1866;* Vol. 2, *The Aristocracy of Sex, 1867–1873.* Edited by Ann D. Gordon. New Brunswick, N.J.: Rutgers University Press, 1997, 2000. (A two-volume anthology of selected papers from the microfilm collection above.)

The Woman's Bible. 2 vols. 1895. Reprint, Amherst, N.Y.: Prometheus, 1999.

BIOGRAPHIES OF ELIZABETH CADY STANTON

Banner, Lois. *Elizabeth Cady Stanton: A Radical for Women's Rights.* Boston: Little, Brown, 1980.

Cullen-DuPont, Kathryn. *Elizabeth Cady Stanton and Women's Liberty.* New York: Facts on File, 1992.

Griffith, Elisabeth. *In Her Own Right: The Life of Elizabeth Cady Stanton.* New York: Oxford University Press, 1984.

BIOGRAPHIES OF OTHER WOMEN'S RIGHTS LEADERS

Bacon, Margaret Hope. *Valiant Friend: The Life of Lucretia Mott.* New York: Walker, 1980.

————. *Mothers of Feminism: The Story of Quaker Women in America.* San Francisco: Harper & Row, 1986. (Includes useful information on Susan B. Anthony, Lucretia Mott, and other Quaker women active in the 19th-century women's rights movement.)

Barry, Kathleen. *Susan B. Anthony: A Biography of a Singular Feminist.* New York: New York University Press, 1988.

Blatch, Harriot Stanton, and Alma Lutz. *Challenging Years: The Memoirs of Harriot Stanton Blatch.* New York: G. P. Putnam's Sons, 1940.

DuBois, Ellen Carol. *Harriot Stanton Blatch and the Winning of Woman Suffrage.* New Haven, Conn.: Yale University Press, 1997. (Includes extensive information on Elizabeth Cady Stanton's personal and public life, especially her relationship with her daughter Harriot.)

Goldsmith, Barbara. *Other Powers: The Age of Suffrage, Spiritualism, and the Scandalous Victoria Woodhull.* New York: Knopf, 1998.

Kerr, Andrea Moore. *Lucy Stone: Speaking Out for Equality.* New Brunswick, N.J.: Rutgers University Press, 1990.

Lasser, Carol, and Marlene Deahl Merrill, eds. *Friends and Sisters: Letters Between Lucy Stone and Antoinette Brown Blackwell, 1846–93.* Urbana: University of Illinois Press, 1987.

Lerner, Gerda. *The Grimké Sisters from South Carolina: Pioneers for Woman's Rights and Abolition.* New York: Oxford University Press, 1998.

Sherr, Lynn, ed. *Failure Is Impossible: Susan B. Anthony in Her Own Words.* New York: Times Books, 1995.

BOOKS ABOUT THE 19TH-CENTURY AMERICAN WOMEN'S RIGHTS MOVEMENT

Braude, Ann. *Radical Spirits: Spiritualism and Women's Rights in Nineteenth-Century America.* Boston: Beacon Press, 1989.

Clinton, Catherine. *The Other Civil War: American Women in the Nineteenth Century.* New York: Hill and Wang, 1984.

DuBois, Ellen. *Feminism and Suffrage: The Emergence of an Independent Women's Movement in America.* Ithaca, N.Y.: Cornell University Press, 1978.

————, ed. *Woman Suffrage and Women's Rights*. New York: New York University Press, 1998.

Flexner, Eleanor. *Century of Struggle: The Women's Rights Movement in the United States*. Cambridge, Mass.: Harvard University Press, 1975.

Frost, Elizabeth, and Kathryn Cullen-DuPont, eds. *Women's Suffrage in America: An Eyewitness History*. New York: Facts on File, 1992.

Hersch, Blanche Glassman. *The Slavery of Sex: Feminist Abolitionists in America*. Urbana: University of Illinois Press, 1978.

Matthews, Jean V. *Women's Struggle for Equality: The First Phase, 1828–1876*. Chicago: Ivan R. Dee, 1997.

Sigerman, Harriet. *An Unfinished Battle: American Women 1848–1865*. New York: Oxford University Press, 1994.

————. *Laborers for Liberty: American Women 1865–1890*. New York: Oxford University Press, 1994.

Smith, Karen Manners. *New Paths to Power: American Women 1890–1920*. New York: Oxford University Press, 1994.

Ryan, Mary P. *Women in Public: Between Banners and Ballots, 1825–1880*. Baltimore: Johns Hopkins University Press, 1990.

Ward, Geoffrey. *Not for Ourselves Alone: The Story of Elizabeth Cady Stanton and Susan B. Anthony, an Illustrated History*. New York: Knopf, 1999.

Weatherford, Doris. *A History of the American Suffragist Movement*. Santa Barbara, Calif.: ABC-Clio, 1998.

INDEX

ACKNOWLEDGMENTS

It takes many people, if not quite a village, to make a book. I first wish to thank Professor Ann Gordon, of the Stanton-Anthony Project, for her very astute reading and critique of the manuscript; her suggestions improved the text immeasurably. Professor Aggie Stillman, the archivist at the Sage Colleges in Troy, New York, graciously spent an afternoon with me talking about Emma Willard and pointed me to some excellent sources. Rhoda Barney Jenkins and Coline Jenkins-Sahlin of the Elizabeth Cady Stanton Trust welcomed me into their homes and generously gave of their time and precious Stanton memorabilia, and I deeply appreciate their enthusiasm and support for this project. Thanks to Fran Antmann for her expert photo research. Brigit Dermott, project editor at Oxford University Press, skillfully guided the manuscript through the many steps to becoming a book, and I thank her for her enthusiasm and deft professionalism. Nancy Toff, editorial director of Trade and Young Adult Reference at Oxford, continues to be an author's best friend and a very special friend to me. And, finally, my husband, Jay L. Banks, came to know Elizabeth Cady Stanton almost as well as I did and remained steadfastly enthusiastic about this project. He is an ardent champion of all that Stanton stood for, and she would have been proud to know him.

PICTURE CREDITS

TEXT CREDITS

p. 52: From *The Selected Papers of Elizabeth Cady Stanton and Susan B. Anthony,* vol. 1, ed. Ann D. Gordon (New Brunswick, N.J.: Rutgers University Press, 1997), 78–79

p. 72: From *The Selected Papers of Elizabeth Cady Stanton and Susan B. Anthony,* vol. 1, ed. Ann D. Gordon (New Brunswick, N.J.: Rutgers University Press, 1997), 402–5

p. 83: From *The Selected Papers of Elizabeth Cady Stanton and Susan B. Anthony,* vol. 1, ed. Ann D. Gordon (New Brunswick, N.J.: Rutgers University Press, 1997), 483–84

p. 122: From *The Elizabeth Cady Stanton–Susan B. Anthony Reader: Correspondence, Writings, Speeches,* ed. Ellen Carol DuBois, rev. ed., (Boston: Northeastern University Press, 1992), 287–89

Harriet Sigerman is a historian and the author of two volumes in the Young Oxford History of Women in the United States, *An Unfinished Battle: American Women 1848–1865* and *Laborers for Liberty: American Women 1865–1890,* and *Land of Many Hands: Women in the American West.* She has also contributed to *European Immigrant Women in the United States: A Biographical Dictionary, The Young Reader's Companion to American History,* and *The American National Biography.* She is a graduate of the University of California at Irvine and holds an M.A. and Ph.D. in American history from the University of Massachusetts at Amherst, where she served as a research assistant for the Stanton–Anthony Papers.